PORTFOLIO

WHAT I DID NOT LEARN AT IIT

Rajeev Agarwal is the founder and the chief executive officer of MAQ Software. Prior to founding MAQ Software in 2000, he worked at Microsoft Corporation, Redmond, for nearly seven years in various product management groups.

MAQ Software has been listed as one of the fastest growing companies in the US eight times—a rare achievement.

Agarwal holds a B.Tech degree in mechanical engineering from IIT Kharagpur, a master's in engineering from Iowa State University, and an MBA from the University of Michigan Business School, Ann Arbor.

He also runs a non-profit organization, Foundation for Excellence, to provide science and mathematics education facilities for girls in rural India.

Agarwal lives in Bellevue, Washington, with his wife, Arpita, and their two children.

Share your success stories at www.IITBook.com. You can contact the author at rajeev@maqsoftware.net.

Praise for the Book

'The world will globalize even further, leading to new opportunities and new challenges. Young professionals will need to build and hone new skills. It will not be their knowledge, but what they do with it that will be important. This book will surely help engineers prepare themselves for professional careers. The book is an easy read and prepares one as they enter the real world.'

SOM MITTAL, **President, NASSCOM**

'*What I Did Not Learn at IIT* is an excellent reflection of Rajeev's constant quest for knowledge and fulfilment. Some of us are fortunate to know Rajeev's humility along with his passion for imbibing knowledge, and this book is representative of both these qualities. It is amazing to see Rajeev share what he has learnt over the years in his successful career with the next generation of people who are entering the workforce—regardless of the route they choose to take. This book is a fantastic, easy read for anyone in different stages of life who seeks to learn and realize their full potential.'

'A much-needed book. The examples are easy to understand and the stories are memorable. Young professionals in many industries will benefit from this book.'

'We are giving copies of this book to our Graduate Engineer Trainees who have joined us from campus this year. Very practical thoughts. Every professional should adopt these in their daily life!'

'An excellent narrative and written in simple language. I read the book in one sitting. Here is an opportunity to enable the "campus hire" hidden within each one of us to make a successful transition to the workplace. A must-read for every young professional who aspires to succeed the right way!'

'It was an easy and quick read. I love the use of checklists. To be honest, I learnt quite a few things reading this book which I will need to incorporate into my work/life. I am planning to make this required reading for my entire team. Great work!'

SHIVA SHENOY, Co-founder and Vice President,
Claims-X-Change

'The examples and ideas mentioned in this book are applicable to almost all industries. Over the last twenty-five years, I have watched Rajeev advance in his own career by practising them. I am certain that these ideas will also help many new graduates advance in their careers. I highly recommend this book.'

O.P. GOYAL, Whole-time Director,
JK Paper Limited

'Having led businesses at global organizations like Wipro, Cisco, EMC and now Mahindra Satyam, I have worked with many successful people. The personal success habits discussed in this book resonate well with me. A must-read for anyone wanting to advance in their career.'

MANOJ CHUGH, Global Head, Business
Development, Enterprise Division, Tech Mahindra

'This authentic and inspiring book will help many young graduates advance in their careers. Many training departments will use this book as a supplement to their own training programmes. A must-read for new graduates if they want to develop successful habits and gain additional perspective on life after college.'

ANKUR PRAKASH, Vice President and Chief Operating Officer, TCS, Latin America

'With many industries suffering from overcapacity, companies in India still have the opportunity to lead the IT services sector. One of the ways to grow a company is to increase the effectiveness of team members. As a Gazelles Growth company, MAQ Software has implemented some of the key growth techniques explained in the book. I highly recommend this book to industry leaders to share with their teams to grow their businesses.'

VERNE HARNISH, Founder and CEO of Gazelles, Inc. and author of *Mastering the Rockefeller Habits*

'This is a great book; it is down to earth, simple in language and uses common sense to explain complex issues. Hopefully, this book will serve as a checklist for a lot of engineers and others to introspect, and improve themselves.'

ARJUN MALHOTRA, Co-founder, HCL Technologies and Headstrong

WHAT I DID **NOT** LEARN AT **IIT**

TRANSITIONING FROM CAMPUS TO WORKPLACE

RAJEEV AGARWAL

PORTFOLIO
PENGUIN

An imprint of Penguin Random House

PORTFOLIO

USA | Canada | UK | Ireland | Australia
New Zealand | India | South Africa | China

Portfolio is part of the Penguin Random House group of companies
whose addresses can be found at global.penguinrandomhouse.com

Published by Penguin Random House India Pvt. Ltd
7th Floor, Infinity Tower C, DLF Cyber City,
Gurgaon 122 002, Haryana, India

First published in Random Business by Random House India 2013
Published in Portfolio by Penguin Random House India 2017

Copyright © Rajeev Agarwal 2013

ISBN 9780143441670

Typeset in Sabon by Saanvi Graphics, Noida
Printed at Thomson Press India Ltd, New Delhi

www.penguin.co.in

Contents

Foreword   xiii

Preface   xvii

1. Introduction   1

2. Transitioning from Campus to the
   Workplace   11

3. Manage Work   24

4. Manage Personal Effectiveness   57

5. Manage Health and Money   96

6. Final Thoughts   123

7. Seven Decisions   125

8. Admirations   127

   Appendix-A: Master Checklist   135

   Appendix-B: Suggested Reading   139

   Appendix-C: E-mail and IM   146

   Appendix-D: Commonly Misused Words   160

Appendix-E: Seven-Minute Exercise   166

Appendix-F: Saving Comparison Details   174

Appendix-G: Appearance   179

Appendix-H: Frequently-Asked Questions 183

Notes   188

About the Author   193

'We are what we repeatedly do.
Excellence, then, is not an act, but a habit.'
— ARISTOTLE

Foreword

When Rajeev, who first worked at Microsoft for many years before becoming a successful entrepreneur, gave me an early draft of this book for input and feedback, the first thing that struck me was Rajeev's passion for wanting to share what he has learned in his career, above and beyond what educational institutions teach you—in his case, IIT; in my case, College of Engineering, Guindy, Anna University.

It got me thinking about what I have learned over the course of my nearly 25-year career since I started at Microsoft—the company I joined directly after graduate school. If I have to summarize the top 3 things that I have learned, they are these:

a) **Follow your heart**—Do what you have passion for as that's when you will strive to do your very best and have the kind of impact that you can and want to have.

b) **Do your very best**—No matter what your current role is, strive to do your best as that will take you places that you never dreamt of or imagined.

c) **Have relentless curiosity and excitement for learning**—That's the best way for you to stay ahead and reach your full potential.

In some sense, like a mirror is a true external reflection of you, what you hold near and dear in terms of values and what you have learned reflects in what you look for in others. At Microsoft, we hire thousands of new employees every year into many kinds of roles and at many levels of seniority. Hiring the best and brightest is critical for Microsoft, and something I am passionate about. Across all the roles at Microsoft, I've noticed that people who exhibit these three ideas tend to be successful. Those who follow their heart have a passion and excitement about their work that energizes their team, their partners, and their customers. Those who strive to do the best they can in their role deliver outstanding results which enable their team to succeed. And those who have a relentless curiosity and excitement for learning are able to adapt to the fast pace of change in the corporate world, particularly in the technology industry. I'm always excited to meet people who are passionate, hard-working, and excited to learn.

One of the most rewarding parts of my job running the Developer Division at Microsoft is to have been a sponsor for the Microsoft Imagine Cup for the last 10 years. The Imagine Cup is the world's premier student technology competition, and has given more than 1.65 million students from across the world the opportunity to learn and create using the most exciting new technologies in the industry. Anyone who knows me understands how passionate I am about encouraging student interest in science and technology, especially, of course, in the Computer Sciences.

Spending time working with students at the Imagine Cup provides a real perspective on the kinds of challenges and opportunities that students face as they transition from campus to the workforce, a theme which Rajeev covers in detail throughout this book. For many of the students, participating in the Imagine Cup is their first experience with new kinds of experiences that the workplace offers; managing time effectively, the importance of teamwork, and a focus on results. This is also their first opportunity to understand what it means to channelize their creativity, energy, and ideas into solutions that can solve real problems for a large number of people around the world. The Imagine Cup has been a great opportunity for me to work with young people who are passionate, excited to learn, curious, and self-starters, and have an amazing work ethic. Seeing these qualities in young people just getting started in technology is exciting. I truly believe it's the dreams and aspirations of these amazing students that will guide each to great success in the near future, and the rest of us confidently into the next phase of technology. As I always say, today's students are tomorrow's leaders. They are going to be running the next generation of businesses, states, and countries.

In this book Rajeev shares his experiences transitioning from IIT to success in the business world. Some of these are experiences I've seen in my own path from university to industry. Others are things I see students experience for the first time at the Imagine Cup every year, or from new employees I work with at Microsoft. And throughout these experiences, you'll see the themes of following your heart, doing your best, and having a relentless curiosity and excitement for learning.

Namaste!

S. Somasegar
Corporate Vice President—Developer Division
Microsoft Corporation

Preface

*'The best way to become acquainted with a subject
is to write a book about it.'*

— BENJAMIN DISRAELI
Former British Prime Minister and novelist

Why did I write the book?
A few years ago, as I finished my company
update to the new graduates, who had just joined, I
was optimistic about the prospects of the company
(the 2008 economic crisis had not hit yet). Many
of the new graduates were eager, motivated, and
excited to hear from me.

After my discussion, one of the graduates cornered
me and asked, 'What is the secret to your success?'
I was speechless. I had never thought about that
question. MAQ Software was a young company
trying to survive in a very competitive market.
Although we were a successful company, I did not
have a ready answer for such a naïve graduate
with such large expectations. She was serious and
expected something like a really thoughtful mantra.
The problem was that success is more than *one* tip.

Not answering wasn't an option, so I gave her a boring answer about discipline and hard work. But her question stayed with me. The answer required explaining many ideas. In fact, to answer the question, I had to write an entire book.

I regularly interact with students, educators, and industry leaders. All three groups blame one another for industry shortfalls. Students say that they lack qualified teachers and college doesn't prepare them for real work. Educators say that students do not study. Industry leaders are disappointed by the quality of graduates produced by our education system. It's a vicious cycle.

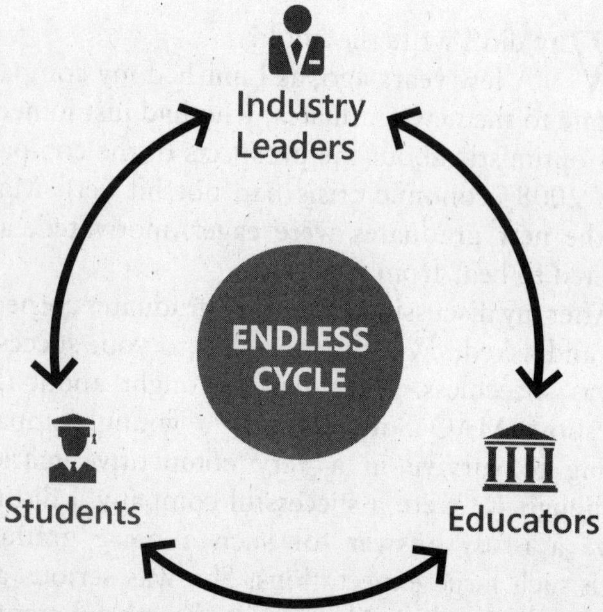

Great students are able to learn despite their teachers. Great institutes see potential and turn average students into superior graduates. Great companies set up great systems to utilize the raw potential of their workforce and deliver great results. Any teacher can turn a high IQ student into a genius. Any student can learn from great teachers. Any company can take IIT graduates and get them to over-deliver. The problem is great teachers and great students and great companies are rare. We never have and we never will have enough of each. As a nation and as a society, our challenge is to take what we have and turn it into what we wish we had.

Instead of facing the issues, we divert our attention to a foreign hand or extend our hand to a foreign land. By sharing my own examples, I hope that in a small way, this book helps to end the blame game.

The reason this book is not titled 'What IIT did not teach me' is that all universities do offer great learning opportunities to all students. Opportunities present themselves in student leadership, academics, sports, music, and many other areas. The river of knowledge is flowing in all academic institutes. It was up to me to recognize and take advantage of these opportunities to grow myself.

I have learned not to give advice. Most people are not looking for advice. Therefore, 'You should' appears only once in this book, and that is right here on this page. I simply share my experiences so that the readers can draw their own conclusions. Most of my recent experiences are related to the software industry. However, some of the ideas may be relevant for other industries.

This book is different in that I wrote it as the active CEO of MAQ Software. This is not a memoir or a reflection of someone long retired. I think that many leaders can share their experiences to serve as positive role models.

'How long have you been working on the book?' a college student recently asked me when I handed him a printed copy. Earnestly, I answered, 'All my life.' While it took me only three months to write the book, it's taken a lot longer to learn and practice the ideas inside.

Many years ago Benjamin Franklin said, 'Either write something worth reading, or do something worth writing.' I hope that you do both.

1

Introduction

'So be sure when you step. Step with care and great
tact. And remember that life's a Great Balancing
Act. Just never forget to be dexterous and deft.
And never mix up your right foot with your left.
And will you succeed? Yes! You will, indeed!
(98 and ¾ percent guaranteed.) Kid, you'll
move mountains.'

—Dr SEUSS, *Oh, The Places You'll Go!*

I graduated from the Indian Institute of Technology
(IIT) over 25 years ago. Since then, I have worked
with hundreds of people across three global
industries—appliances, software, and consulting. I
have worked with many engineers who rose through
the ranks quickly, while many others took much
longer.

In working with all of these people, I observed
a common pattern of success. People who are
successful in any area of life—whether it is politics,
sports, business, or academics—share common
behaviours and habits.

I look back and see that my own journey became easier once I realized it was better to follow the pattern followed by successful people. Once I consistently started adopting these common traits and behaviours, it was easy to succeed.

This book contains my knowledge, observations, and reflections based on my industry experience and my interactions with many professionals. As I discuss these topics, I maintain a learning mindset and continue to learn. I hope you will benefit from these insights as you move forward in your career.

Perspective

Most of these ideas have been around for centuries, and they will probably be around for centuries more. Working hard and being proactive are not new ideas.

If we are anything like our parents' generation, most of us will not be able to retire until we are 65-years-old. That means that after we leave college, 40 years of work lies ahead for most of us.

When I was in college, I was focussed on securing a good job after graduation. At the entry level, most employers hire engineers because they possess technical knowledge. However, success requires more than technical knowledge. Having grown up in Shahjahanpur, Uttar Pradesh, a small district town with an agriculture-based economy, I did not learn many of the professional skills needed to be successful in a knowledge-based economy.

Several factors probably limited my own professional growth:

1. Typical of most families, my parents and people in my hometown assumed that since I had gotten into IIT, I would automatically be successful. They assumed that the Mathematics, Physics, and Chemistry required for entry into IIT was sufficient for a successful career.

2. When I entered college, I mistakenly assumed there was only one path to success. I learned there are many paths to success; there is no one formula or mantra. Some of the advice we receive is even contradictory. Some successful people dropped out of college, while others secured an MBA. Should I drop out of college or should I finish my degree? The only lesson I could draw from all of this was that what works for me may not work for you. All of us have a different starting point in life; all of us have unique strengths, weaknesses, and opportunities.

3. I surrounded myself with people who had short-term orientation (which meant, 'What movie or cricket match are we watching this weekend?'). I did not know how to resolve the tension between managing short-term expectations while thinking about my long-term career.

Unknown to me during my high school and IIT years, the world was globalizing very rapidly. At the time, India's economy was not open to foreign investments. Similar to many emerging markets, the government placed a huge emphasis on self-reliance and avoided imports.

In May 1995, legendary Harvard Professor John P. Kotter published the results of a longitudinal study of Harvard MBAs. As a part of the study, he studied 115 members of Harvard Business School's Class of 1974 for over 20 years.

In his book, *The New Rules: How to Succeed in Today's Post-corporate World,*[1] Professor Kotter describes how the oil crisis of 1973 altered career paths, wage levels, the structure and functioning of corporations, and the nature of work itself.

Although a lot has changed since he conducted his research, Kotter showed that conventional career paths through 'large corporations no longer automatically lead to success' as they once did (New Rule #1). He explains that globalization is creating 'new opportunities for those with education, motivation, and talent' (New Rule #2) and large hazards for others who fear competition and overvalue security.

Through year-by-year analysis of the choices, actions, successes, and failures of the 115 MBAs, Kotter documented that the greatest opportunities had 'shifted away from large bureaucratic companies to smaller or more entrepreneurial ones' (New Rule #3). Kotter concludes that those who are successful show 'a willingness to continue to learn' over an entire lifetime (New Rule #8).

Chaos and Uncertainty

Since the publication of *The New Rules*, the Internet appeared and everything changed again. As Kotter predicted, globalization, facilitated by advances in telecommunication, created enormous opportunities. Huge companies were created. Since then, the dot-com boom was followed by the dot-com bust, and we have had several global economic crises. Experts are now saying that the turbulence we have seen in the past 15 years is the *new normal*. We should plan for and embrace that new reality.

When I was an MBA student at the University of Michigan, there was a huge emphasis on globalization trends. But there was no way I could understand its impact at the time. I never imagined that I would be part of a company that has a globally distributed workforce working in two time zones nearly 12 hours apart.

Many countries, including India, have benefited tremendously from the globalization of industries. Low-cost Internet bandwidth and cheaper computing enabled work to take place anywhere in the world. And the pace of change is only increasing as globalization increases.

Today, when I talk to senior managers in almost any industry, they face commoditization of products and services. Their profit margins are shrinking. Senior managers tell me, 'Look, everybody is selling the same thing, and our only differentiator is price.'

With those two driving factors—increased global competition and commoditization of products and services—the role of leadership at every level has become more important. As Jim Collins mentions in *Good to Great*,[2] a few practices are common among great companies. They hire disciplined people. They practice disciplined thought. They act in a disciplined manner. Overnight success may take 25 years or more to achieve.

New Framework (Dhancha)

Pulitzer Prize winning author Thomas Friedman describes globalization's impact on countries in *The Lexus and the Olive Tree*.[3] In his book, Friedman says that countries have to wear a Golden Straitjacket. According to Wikipedia, a straitjacket is a garment shaped like a jacket with long sleeves. The straightjacket provides no flexibility to the person wearing it. A straightjacket is typically used to restrain a person who may otherwise cause harm to himself or others.

With the Golden Straitjacket, there is increased uniformity across nations. Our policies, rules, practices, economy, and resulting lifestyle are defined and enforced with the world as a whole, rather than just within the context of our own countries. Friedman describes how nations are being forced to reduce the size of government, reduce subsidies, privatize public-sector companies, reduce import taxes (duties), and reduce inflation. To attract investors and create jobs, countries must follow a strict framework or pattern of government. Countries that do not open their economy to global trade are left behind in poverty.

As individuals, we have to adopt the new 'dhancha' (IT Jacket) or wear the Golden Straitjacket. As we struggle to change, we are forced to adopt the new rules. For most of us, change is hard. I myself do not like to change, even if it's for a simple thing like tea. As I travel from Delhi to Mumbai to Hyderabad, tea is served differently. I still like my chai the way it was served in my formative years at home and at Kharagpur.

In our own minds, in the minds of our families, and in the mind of our society, we are conflicted. Our parents' generation has different expectations and aspirations than our generation. After IIT, my family would have liked me to return to my hometown, find a job there, get married, and stay there. I did not see any job opportunities in my hometown. Besides, I had different aspirations. Most young people face this conflict where they have to make important choices that influence our successes and failures.

We have to manage the conflict between the two generations. Whether and how fast to adopt the new dhancha? Can we choose some aspects from the old and some aspects from the new? Can we mix and match? Can we have the best of both worlds?

TABLE 1.1: HOW OUR WORKPLACE HAS CHANGED IN THE PAST 20 YEARS

Workplace	Old Pattern	New Dhancha
Location	Hometown, certainly home state	Bangalore, Pune, Mumbai, Delhi, Hyderabad, and Chennai
Office Language	Hindi or native language. English optional	English. Native language optional
Workweek	Six-day workweek	Five-day workweek
Job Security	Assured job for life	Limited job security
Office Culture	Easy-going	Fast paced, demanding
Workspace	Older offices with fans, typewriters	AC offices with computers, cafeteria
Income	Low by global standards	Comparable after adjusting for cost of living
Retirement	Pension	No such thing
Taxes	High income tax rates, low compliance. Evade taxes	Form 16, PAN number. Lower tax rate, higher tax payment. Not easy to evade taxes

TABLE 1.2: HOW OUR LIFESTYLE HAS CHANGED IN THE PAST 20 YEARS

Lifestyle	Old Pattern	New Dhancha
Family	Joint family	Independent
Health	No insurance	Health insurance
Telephone, Internet	Landline (did not work)	Cell phone (who needs a landline?)
Food	Traditional only	Traditional + fast food (Pizza, McDonald's)
Transport	Bus and non AC trains	Airplanes, AC trains, and cars
Shopping	Local merchant	Malls and online
News	Government controlled. AIR and Doordarshan	Everything but AIR and Doordarshan

Many 22-year-old engineers earn more than double the income of their parents who have worked for nearly 30 to 40 years. Parents used to be astonished. Now, parents expect a high salary for their graduate children. What many parents do not realize is that the new salary requires their graduate children to adopt the new dhancha. Many families want us to have the benefits of the new salary but not the pain from adopting the new dhancha.

Many of us are suddenly thrown into a globalized work environment with a very different set of expectations. While we are happy to accept the higher pay and glitzy work environment, we do not want to wear the IT jacket. The IT jacket requires us to adopt new behaviours to meet expectations from our employers. The new dhancha, or the IT jacket, requires us to know English, move away from joint families, move to metro cities, keep our skills current, pay income tax, and work with people from all over India and the world.

Many new skills, behaviours, and habits are needed to be successful in the globalized workforce. The sooner we get acclimated to the dhancha, the faster we can adopt it.

Despite all of the challenges, we have made a lot of progress as a nation. Many of us have adapted well to the new dhancha. As a result, our economy and gross domestic product (GDP) is significantly larger. Our standard of living has improved.

We are a country of successful people, and our industry is filled with great people. I am sure you are already successful, and you'll be more successful moving forward. By sharing my experiences, my intent is to make sure all of you are successful over the *long-term*—40 years and not just till next month.[4]

2

Transitioning from Campus to the Workplace

'I was born not knowing and have had only a little time to change that here and there.'

—RICHARD FEYNMAN
Winner, Nobel Prize for Physics

In my final year at IIT Kharagpur, I was offered a Trainee Engineer job with Maruti Suzuki. In the early eighties, only about 20,000 cars were licensed to be manufactured every year in India. Through a joint venture with the Government of India, Suzuki Motor Corporation, Japan, had set up a brand-new car manufacturing plant on the outskirts of Delhi. Using the latest engineering techniques, the plant was set to manufacture 100,000 cars per year. By early 1986, the plant had started producing 50,000 cars annually and was in the early stages of sourcing components locally.

At only 47,000 rupees, early Maruti Suzuki 800 cars were priced well below their Fiat and

Ambassador competitors. The car industry was taking a major leap forward and catching up with the latest offerings from Japan. Competing Indian car models had not been updated for decades due to low production volumes and restrictions on manufacturing licenses. But times were changing.

Suzuki Motors sent about 200 Japanese specialists to help set up the plant and run the operations initially. Maruti Suzuki had hired 25 mechanical engineers exclusively from IITs to build an engineering team in India to design new cars for the Indian market. I coveted the job because of the excitement surrounding the upcoming car, and the opportunity to work at the state-of-the-art manufacturing plant. A posting in Gurgaon, located outside New Delhi, was convenient for me because of the north India location. As a Trainee Engineer, I was offered a stipend and a shared accommodation.

When I reported to work at Maruti Suzuki on Monday, May 26, 1986, at Gurgaon, Haryana, I was amazed at the size of the manufacturing plant and the assembly line. As an engineering student at Kharagpur, I had visited TELCO's (now called Tata Motors) truck manufacturing plant and steel manufacturing (TISCO, now called Tata Steel) plants at the nearby town of Jamshedpur. I had also visited Metal Box's (now called Tata Bearings) local ball bearing manufacturing plant at Kharagpur. During my third year summer internship, I had worked at the Eicher Motors tractor research and development centre.

The Maruti Suzuki plant was different; it was a brand-new manufacturing plant. It was free of grease and oil spots on the shop floor, and free of the clutter I had seen in the other plants. Everything was well organized and properly kept. All needed items were easily available and each item had a purpose or utility.

The design engineering team was run by a General Manager named A.G. Deshpande who had recently returned from West Germany to lead the efforts. An ex-military trainer named P.K. Sharma was in charge of our training. My experience at Maruti Suzuki was very different from my college experience and my expectations from work after leaving school. I was used to classroom education, and I had never expected to learn so much about cars by working on an assembly line.

Following the Japanese management style, there were no private offices for anyone, including the General Manager. The entire engineering team office followed an open floor plan, which facilitated collaboration and osmotic communication among employees. Conference rooms were available for private meetings with some reserved for senior managers. To signify uniformity, we were given grey uniforms with grey caps. The only difference between the supervisors and non-supervisors was that the supervisors had blue caps. Everyone, including the assembly line workers, ate the same food in the same cafeteria.

As a mechanical engineer, I had studied internal combustion engines, thermodynamics, and fluid mechanics. But despite being from a reputed institute, I did not know anything about cars. Most of my fellow engineers were in a similar situation. During my summer at Maruti Suzuki, I learned about inducting new engineers to the company. The training was very relevant and rigorous.

Following the Japanese induction technique, I was assigned to work on the assembly line. This was done to ensure that I knew the different parts of the car and how they were assembled. It was not necessarily the most comfortable experience— summer in north India is very hot, and temperatures can reach up to 45 degrees centigrade.

To maximize learning, each trainee engineer worked on a station and replaced an assembly line worker. We rotated to a new station every week to learn about a different part of the car. The job at one of my first assembly stations was to perfectly install a windshield on a car every few minutes. Any worker had the authority to press a red button and stop the assembly line in case there was a problem. This approach displayed empowerment to the employees and resulted in higher quality. We were careful with our work and did our work right the first time. We were focussed on the work at hand and produced great quality cars. We rarely used the option to stop the assembly line since it impacted production goals for the day and invited an unpleasant visit from the plant manager.

While assembling cars, I learned a lot about Japanese production systems, and how to design harnesses and assembly stations. I learned that it is possible to install a windshield without any complex tool. I used only a simple rope to fit the glass screen on the car. I still marvel at their superior manufacturing engineering and how they kept everything simple. There was only one way to assemble the car, and it was difficult to assemble incorrectly. Through improved design techniques, the company limited the number and type of different nuts and bolts.

One common problem other companies' manufacturing plants faced was the regular shortage of correct parts. The second problem was using incorrect parts to assemble a car. At Maruti Suzuki, many parts were interchangeable so assembly was easy and assembly mistakes were avoided.

Many years later, when I started my own company, I found that many ideas used to assemble cars were equally applicable to producing software. We adapted many engineering practices from Japanese management techniques. New employee training is very rigorous and relevant, and everyone is required to complete it regardless of their position. New engineers set up their own computers with software. To help build their confidence and familiarity with their computer hardware, new engineers assemble their own personal computers (PC). Next, the engineers install their Operating System and install development tools and utilities from the beginning. Despite holding a four-year Electronics Engineering or Computer Science degree from a reputed institute, many engineers have never assembled a personal computer. They have never changed a failed hard disk or installed a memory module in a PC—a very simple procedure.

Similar to producing cars, many companies design software test harnesses and assembly procedures. These techniques ensure that there is only one correct way to design and deploy software to production. To facilitate teamwork and reduce communication gaps, many leading companies such as Intel, Google, and Facebook utilize open floor plans.

Transitioning from a college environment to a job can be a challenge. My own story is typical of many graduates. Early in my career, I moved from one milestone to the next without recognizing a broader pattern. That meant passing high school, then intermediate school, finishing IIT, and then securing a job. I did not realize that after I left college to start working in a company, I needed to change again to adapt to the new environment.

Moving into the workplace, I faced a new set of rules, a new set of relationships, and a new structure that was based on experience and skills. In a way, it was similar to my transition from intermediate school to engineering college.

Unlike the university atmosphere, there is a lot of competition among companies in any industry. Companies are constantly trying to improve their products and services to multiply profits by increasing market share and reducing costs. After all, investors do not want to invest in a company whose share price is not increasing. As a result, the atmosphere within any company is quite competitive.

Recently, the *Economic Times* reported that every year over one lakh (115,711) Computer Science/IT engineers graduate in India.[5] In addition, there are two lakh (200,000) Electronics/Mechanical/Chemical, and Civil Engineering graduates who aspire for a job in the IT industry.

Despite the growth of IT, it is unlikely that so many net new jobs will be created every year. Because there will be more graduates than openings, engineering graduates will have to compete to get these jobs and compete to advance in their companies.

A similar article[6] on rediff.com from January 31, 2013, mentioned that with 4,500 colleges in India offering MBA programs, there are 360,000 seats. With the exception of the top 20 schools, only 10 percent of graduates get placed after graduating. Around 180 MBA colleges closed in 2012 and 160 colleges are expected to close in 2013. An oversupply of fresh graduates is creating a very difficult job environment for the unprepared.

It is important to study the competitive environment and not be afraid of competition. I competed to get into a good engineering college. I competed to get a job in a good company. And I competed to get selected for good projects. Similarly, successful graduates enjoy the competition and strive to always stay ahead of the curve. Team members are constantly observing my interactions, my presentations, the e-mail messages I send, and my Facebook posts. Similarly, managers are constantly judging team members on their interactions, both verbal and non-verbal. Superiors judge how you dress, how you talk, and how you behave.

When graduates start a new job, they enter a competitive environment.

Supervisors Are Generalists, Not Specialists

I am certain that you've met many people who think that they know much better than their superiors. When we are new to the workplace, it is natural for many of us to resent our managers. Early in my career, I had many supervisors who did not have the same level of technical depth as me. I felt that I knew better.

However, supervisors, as they gain industry experience and get promoted, have worked across different technologies, different projects, and different types of project roles (development, testing, project management, etc.). Supervisors become generalists as opposed to being specialists in one technology (say, Java). Specializing in one technology is generally not enough to get one to a managerial role.

For example, someone may know more about JavaScript, but their supervisor knows more about Software Development Life Cycle (SDLC), Continuous Delivery, other projects in the company, IT industry, and/or client domain.

While it seems unfair, I realize now, that is how the workplace is designed. I came to understand that my manager may not know everything I may know about the project. However, if I am working for a successful company, chances are that the selection of my manager was a deliberate decision. I may not agree with the decision, but I have to live with it.

Success in Projects Differs from Success in Exams

Working on software development as a career is very different from sitting for an exam for three hours. With an exam, we get only one attempt to show our knowledge and best work. We cannot change our exam scores ever. In contrast, with project work, we can spend more time perfecting our work. For example, on software projects, we get an opportunity to re-do our work on a continuous basis by releasing a new software build every day.

Most exams are designed to test an individual's knowledge. As a result, we have to take exams by ourselves. By contrast, in most companies projects are completed by a team and not just by an individual. While we are doing our work, we can refer to previous projects and consult other co-workers. We can refer to previous mistakes (bugs) in past projects. We can refer to books and websites for new ideas and techniques.

As a result of these differences, I have seen many talented engineers with average academic records do very well. These successful individuals were pro-active, resourceful, and ingenious problem solvers.

Instead of taking an 'all or nothing' approach to developing a functionality, the successful project teams develop functionality incrementally. These teams develop a prototype (proof of concept), which demonstrates the feasibility and technical approach. If the approach is wrong, they find failures early and save time and effort. Next a program is written to handle error scenarios and corner cases. Over time, these teams continue to refine their implementation and refactor the software code multiple times.

Life Isn't Fair—But Only in the Short Term

> 'All the adversity I've had in my life, all my troubles and obstacles, have strengthened me... You may not realize it when it happens but a kick in the teeth may be the best thing in the world for you.'
>
> —WALT DISNEY
> Founder of The Walt Disney Company

Many of us feel that life is not fair. But that is true only in the short term. We think, 'That person is getting promoted. He's so lucky.' That is life. I did not always get the performance review, the great boss, or the choice project I felt I deserved. These things have happened to me as well and to many other people I know.

My rule of thumb is that if you work for 10 years in your life, chances are that for 3 years of your work life you will say, 'I wish I did not have this job, or this project, or this company.' Seven years out of those 10 years will be quite good. The problem is that we don't know going forward which 3 years will not be great.[7]

For almost any company, if I pick the last 10 years, 3 years were not really that great. In hindsight, we only know that 3 years did not turn out to be great. But these companies couldn't pick those 3 years beforehand. They couldn't say, 'Okay, these 3 years are not going to go as well as planned. Let's not have those 3 years.' That's how it worked out for me.

In my experience, most good people do well in the long term. Most managers recognize good employees and reward them appropriately when a new opportunity is available.

Leaders Stay with their Company or Industry

When I look at any company or any industry, many of the CEOs have spent a long time with their companies. They rose to the top over time as they pitched in to build their respective companies.

When I work with fresh MBA graduates, I ask them to study leadership in a few industries. Invariably, whichever industry they select, they find that key leaders have been with their companies for over 20 years.

If you frequently switch companies or industries, the transition between them can be difficult. When I changed groups or employers, I had to start over and build my credibility with the new team all over again. Transitioning requires extra time and effort. Instead, it is better to invest time in one company and grow with it as the experience counts and you are better rewarded for it.

For reference, below is a list of the CEOs of some leading IT services companies, their tenure, and their background:

- ⚜ N. Chandrashekhar, CEO at TCS
  - ◇ With TCS since 1987
  - ◇ 26 years with the company
  - ◇ MCA from REC, Trichy
- ⚜ T.K. Kurien, CEO at Wipro
  - ◇ With Wipro since 2001, associated earlier with Wipro/GE Medical collaboration
  - ◇ 12 years with the company
  - ◇ Chartered Accountant
- ⚜ Pierre Nanterme, CEO at Accenture
  - ◇ With Accenture since 1983
  - ◇ 30 years with the company
- ⚜ Virginia Rometty, CEO at IBM Global Services
  - ◇ With IBM since 1981
  - ◇ 32 years with the company
  - ◇ Bachelor of Computer Science, North-western University
- ⚜ Anant Gupta, CEO at HCL

◇ With HCL since 1994
◇ 19 years with the company
◇ MS from the University of Liverpool

Most of these CEOs faced several years of turmoil and economic uncertainty over the twenty odd years at their companies. When a tough assignment came up, they raised their hand. They got out of their comfort zone. Instead of changing companies, they chose to grow with the company.

Checklist for Campus to Workplace Transition

✤ Learn about the department and the company

✤ Speak to alumni in the company and city

✤ Review core subjects in Computer Science, including Data Structures and Databases

3

Manage Work

'It is not work that kills men, it is worry. Work is healthy; you can hardly put more on a man than he can bear. But worry is rust upon the blade. It is not movement that destroys the machinery, but friction.'

—HENRY WARD BEECHER
American clergyman and abolitionist

The culture and work environment in a company is influenced by many factors. In my experience, the work environment depends on the kind of work that goes on in the company. The nature of work at the company decides the kind of people the company hires and retains. The nature of output (work) dictates the kind of processes that are followed by the company. Geographic location can also affect operating conditions and culture. For example, the software industry in India is relatively young. Visitors from outside India are surprised to find so many young people (below the age of 30) managing so many large teams in most IT companies. In more mature industries, the managers are much older and more experienced.

As I observe our engineers who are successful and get promoted young, they share many common traits. One of them is managing their time at work in a way that is more productive than their colleagues.

Along with the constant need to learn and adopt new technologies, many of us struggle with spending long hours at work. When we survey our employees, most concerns are about long work hours.

Forty Hours Is a Long Time to Work

In my view, 40 hours per week, if you're working in a focussed manner, is a long time to work. Most of us cannot really work for 40 hours a week. Most projects are staffed to accommodate unplanned events, unproductive meetings, absent employees, and malfunctioning equipment. The fact is that most companies cannot generate work for you for 40 hours.

Then why do we spend 60 hours a week in the office? There are many reasons. The first is poor management. Work has not been organized correctly and no one has thought about how to allocate that work. The second reason usually involves all of the distractions that are present in our workplace. They include our constant need to keep up with personal and work e-mails, text messages, websites, Facebook posts, instant messages, and phone calls. The result is that you are constantly switching between tasks.

This is known as 'task-switching', as opposed to 'multitasking', or working on multiple tasks simultaneously (which is impossible for humans).[8] Task-switching creates an environment for technical mistakes and miscommunication.

Over the years, I have learned to control my task-switching. I have become more disciplined. For instance, I avoid immediately answering all of my phone calls—I prefer to use voice mail. I also do not immediately respond to an e-mail unless it is from a customer or superior. I am also selective about my personal phone calls at work and while not at work.

ENJOY THE WORK

When I was an MBA student, I took many required classes on Organizational Behaviour (OB). During my first semester as an MBA student, I took OB 501—one of the core classes required for all MBA students. The class was taught by Professor Jane Dutton. Being an engineer, I did not have any background in solving problems that did not have only *one right answer* and that required judgment, not technique. I was fascinated by the OB 501 class and the cases we discussed. Over the years, these classes have helped in every workplace situation and in putting many things into perspective.

In one of the classes, Professor Dutton discussed a conversation she had had with a Ford Motor Company executive. She had asked him what she could teach her MBA students that would make them more effective at Ford. The auto executive replied that what he needed could not be taught by her. He needed students who were *passionate* about cars. They should love cars. They should get excited about cars. The business skills that students pick up in gaining their MBAs are important, but passion for automobiles was the most important quality Ford was looking for.

For most of my career, I have enjoyed working with software. When a new version of an Operating System is released, I am the first one to install it. Since I enjoy software, work does not seem like work. This is a classic example of something that cannot be learned at an institute, no matter how prestigious.

NOT ALL EMPLOYERS ARE THE SAME

Even though two companies may operate in the same industry, they can be very different. When I speak with people who have worked for other IT companies, I am surprised to find different cultures and vastly different operating practices. In a large company, the culture can vary from one division or operating unit to another.

In the following table, I've contrasted the cultural differences across organizations that may exist due to the nature of work performed. Similar examples exist in almost all industries.

TABLE 3.1: DIFFERENT TYPES OF ORGANIZATIONS IN THE IT INDUSTRY

Career	Progressive Organizations	Traditional IT Service Providers
Culture	Entrepreneurial	Bureaucratic
Work	70% work on new applications, smaller projects	70% work on maintenance and support, larger projects
Technologies	Anything older than 2 years is obsolete	Likely to be older systems
Processes	Agile and Daily Build Model (CMMi not relevant)	CMMi and highly restrictive processes
People	Computer Science/IT degree required	Most engineering streams accepted
Idle Engineers (bench)	Less than 10%, cannot afford idle employees	30–50% of India employees on bench (72–75% utilization)
Growth/Learning	High due to rich work experience on projects	Low growth and limited learning due to repetitive work

For many computer software engineers, their knowledge is obsolete as soon as they leave the university. Most progressive organizations focus on creating a rich learning environment. With the rapid advances in technologies, traditional organizations have, sometimes painfully, had to adjust. As a technology services provider, the benefits of technological advances cannot be delivered to our clients if we do not change faster than the industry.

E-MAIL

New graduates must recognize that e-mail (Outlook) and instant messaging (Lync) are formal methods of communication. Most new graduates are not familiar with using Microsoft Outlook for e-mail, contacts, and calendar since it is rarely used in engineering colleges. However, most companies use Microsoft Office extensively. As a result, Microsoft Outlook is the standard e-mail program in most companies. While every company and industry uses e-mail differently, most engineers spend at least 1–2 hours every day working with Microsoft Outlook. Many organizations work hard to ensure that the new engineers know how to use Microsoft Outlook efficiently.

Many new graduates write an e-mail as if they are writing a text message to a friend, resulting in a poor impression. It is important for new engineers to learn how to send e-mail messages that are professional. Well-written e-mail messages take time to write. In my e-mails, I avoid slang and spelling mistakes by using the built-in tools in Outlook.

When I work with new engineers, I find that many do not respond to an e-mail until they have completed the work or found a solution. Today, most people expect e-mail messages to be acknowledged the same day. Most of our managers and clients find a same-day response acceptable. I find it troubling when many new graduates wait to respond to an e-mail message for a few days until they have the complete answer. I find it useful to send a simple message stating that I received their message and I am working on the request. I also let the sender know when to expect a complete response.

Not all e-mail messages are of equal importance. I do come across people and situations where a response is expected immediately. When I was working at Microsoft, if the CEO sent an e-mail, most managers ensured that a detailed and accurate response was provided within hours. A lot of the protocol in a company is industry and people specific. I use my best judgment to balance responsiveness with distractions.

Plenty of material is available on proper e-mail etiquette online. I have listed some of my common observations and techniques in Appendix-C. I regularly refer to the list to remind myself of the best practices.

Multitasking is a Lie

Multitasking is our attempt to simultaneously do as many things as quickly as possible, generally using the power of many technologies. Now-a-days cell phone advertisements suggest that we can use technology to accomplish several things at once. I have seen many resumes where job candidates use the word 'multitasking' in the 'skills' sections of their résumés.

However, it has been widely documented that multitasking is a myth.[9] In our brain, we are switching from being present in the meeting to processing e-mail, from talking to our co-worker to commenting on Facebook. Task-switching is not very efficient. We simply cannot multitask.

I attend a lot of meetings where attendees are processing their e-mail while they are in a meeting. These attendees are switching tasks between listening to a conversation and checking and replying to e-mails. Some attendees even send text messages. This is task-switching where my mind switches from one task to another. It is not possible to pay equal attention and do justice to two tasks at the same time.

Dr Edward Hallowell, a Massachusetts-based psychiatrist, calls multitasking a 'mythical activity in which people believe they can perform two or more tasks simultaneously'. In January 2005, he published an article in the *Harvard Business Review* called 'Overloaded Circuits: Why Smart [Intelligent] People Underperform.' In the article, Hallowell describes a new condition known as Attention Deficit Trait (ADT) which he claims is common in the business world. ADT is marked by distractibility, inner frenzy, and impatience. Hallowell cautions that ADT is not an illness or character defect, it's just our brains' natural response to trying to handle too much information. ADT is different from Attention Deficit Disorder (ADD) which is a neurological disorder whose causes include a genetic component.

Environmental and physical factors may increase ADD symptoms. By contrast, ADT is caused by us and does not have a genetic component.

ADT's bad effects can be controlled only by managing our environment and our emotional and physical health. Limiting task and context switching is essential. Hallowell provides several strategies for overcoming ADT. For example, setting aside e-mail until we have completed one or two more important tasks. Breaking large tasks into smaller ones. Asking a colleague to help us stop talking on the telephone, e-mailing, or working too late. Free computer programs like StayFocusd may help us limit the amount of time spent on time-wasting websites. For some of us, these monitoring tools can help us avoid distractions.

I do one thing at a time. I make fewer mistakes. My work is of better quality. As a result, I found that I am less frenzied. As soon as I enter the elevator, I am not hitting the door close button again and again to save time.

Avoid Distractions at Work

'It is not enough to be busy. So are the ants. The question is: What are we busy about?'

—HENRY DAVID THOREAU
American philosopher

In our fast-moving world of instant news, instant messages, e-mail, Facebook, blogs, etc., it is easy to get distracted. Distractions can become an addiction. Distractions activate the same part of the brain as cocaine does.[10] Recent research shows that if we switch tasks, it takes us another 25 minutes before our focus on the initial task returns. We are more likely to make mistakes and spend more time correcting them.

Some of the common distractions found at work that negatively impact us include:

- Instant Messenger
- cell phone
- listening to music
- Skype log-on notifications
- checking Facebook posts
- Twitter
- e-mail
- sending and responding to text messages

Earlier this year, one of our teams decided to voluntarily adopt a 'distraction-free hour'. Every day, they turned off cell phones, Outlook, and Skype for an hour. The team reported a significant increase in their ability to get their work done in a shorter time. They were able to go home earlier. Since unfinished work causes stress, they also reported a higher level of satisfaction from work completion.[11]

Certain Jobs Are Time-consuming

In my experience, I have found that certain roles and jobs are time-consuming. For example, if you are supervising people, or are on the HR team, it is difficult to be efficient. You cannot be efficient with people. People want to talk; they want to be heard; and they want to be understood. Dealing with people takes time.

Most knowledge-work job roles require a lot of creativity and judgment. When we are doing creative work, we have to research, evaluate, and develop efficient solutions. A lot of knowledge-work takes a long time. Similar to management jobs that require long hours, most medical doctors I know are required to work very long hours. Most medical students and interns spend 80 hours or more every week at the hospital during their 3 years of medical residency programs.

Similarly, software development, management consulting, and IT industry jobs are time-consuming and may take longer than planned. The management consulting industry requires long hours and significant amounts of travel for most people. I was not willing to travel every week. Because of this, when I was graduating from my MBA program, I did not apply for a job with any consulting company despite their high salaries.

Software jobs require long hours because the industry and software systems are not mature. Many software systems are new and are constantly changing. These systems have many moving parts and changing components. Many programs are being written for the first time. Whenever we do something for the first time, it takes us longer compared to something repetitive that we have already done 50 times.

For example, in the last 20 years I have installed operating systems on personal computers over 500 times. Through the years, the speed and usability of hardware and software has improved. Sometimes I need only 10 minutes to install the operating system on a PC. But at other times, I have spent 5–6 hours installing the same operating system on a similar but slightly different computer. The huge variations in time come from several factors. Sometimes the variation is caused by improper device drivers, sometimes it's due to faulty computer hardware, and sometimes due to my own errors and unfamiliarity with the software. I find software addictive and stay to finish the installation. I do not leave till I find the answer and the cause of the problem.

I have come across situations where a program we wrote and tested on our own computer system doesn't run on the customer's system the next day. We have to then investigate and find the problem. The length of time needed to solve the problem depends on its complexity. It also depends on the skill of the person tasked with solving it. Sometimes the problem can be solved in a few minutes. Sometimes it may take us days to resolve.

Once I understand the nature and demands of the job role, it is easier to set my own expectations and decide accordingly.

Work Gets Easier with Experience

Several industry studies have shown that an experienced engineer can be three times more productive than an inexperienced engineer. Often, we do not have the experience necessary to do our work in the most efficient way. Sometimes, lack of productivity is due to unfamiliarity with the tools, poor setup of the operating environment, or limited understanding of the client domain.

Over time, as our engineers become proficient in development tools, they reorganize the operating environment and gain customer knowledge. We have seen that the work becomes significantly easier and more satisfying.

Plan Ahead

Though spontaneous plans are exciting for some, I find them stressful. When it comes to the workplace, it is much better for me to plan in advance so that other team members can plan their work around my schedule. I plan my day and week ahead as much as possible. I have also learned to plan my year in advance. For example, our company calendar is published for the coming 12 months on a rolling basis.

Advance planning simplifies my life and the schedules of those around me. This simple technique has helped me significantly, since my yearly travel plan is dictated by the calendar. When planning one year in advance, some people feel constrained. However, I look at myself as getting freed up because I can fit my daily schedule to the yearly calendar. Planning has certainly helped me become more successful.

In our first few years as a startup company, we did not have a fixed calendar. We did not even have fixed annual events. Now, we set dates for our annual events and rarely change them. We strongly encourage our engineers to plan their holidays and personal events around key company meetings.

ATTEND COMPANY EVENTS

In any company calendar, there are only 5 or 6 days when important events are held (e.g., Annual Employee Picnic, Quarterly Information Meeting, and Communication Training). Many of these events are hosted by senior managers to share important information and to meet people. Many topics are discussed at a high level. Professionals can gain insights from the speakers at the events.

I find that many young professionals skip these events in favor of their personal or social engagements. These 5 or 6 days constitute only 1.5 percent of the days in a year. Many young professionals do not attend because they think these events have little relevance to their everyday work. But these events are very relevant. The amount of time allotted to a speaker or a topic may indicate the importance of a person or an area in the coming year. Young professionals can also observe the speakers, their way of discussing the industry, their choice of words, and their dress. Furthermore, not attending the event sends a signal to the company's managers that someone is not interested and may not be around for long. Employees' absence implies that they have stopped participating and are investing only the bare minimum to keep their jobs.

Track Items to Closure

When I was in college, my professors gave me weekly assignments and graded them on a regular basis. They provided the structure and tracked my work. They penalized me for not turning in my work on time and for incorrectly completing it. When I started working as an engineer, the work was less structured. In a typical company there are many open-ended work items, and project timelines extend to multiple months or years. Usually, the supervisors do not have time to chase everyone on a daily basis. As an employee, I had to learn to track my own work items that included following up with co-workers.

Making sure an action item gets done is crucial. Today, when I am working on corporate development projects, it is my job to follow up on work items with the concerned team members. For my projects, I follow up on a daily basis to ensure that no one is blocked and work items are being completed.

Once an item has been completed, I advise every-one to check to ensure that the work has been done satisfactorily. This simple technique avoids communication gaps and any mismatch in expectations between us and our clients.

For example, every time I talk to the project management team, I focus on key quarterly priorities. I follow up repeatedly—usually every week—to ensure that work items have been completed. I have seen many good engineers lose track of work items and not follow through. As a result, some engineers, despite their superior technical skills, find themselves unable to complete projects. I like to use simple checklists to keep track of my work items.

It is also important to know when an item is done. Otherwise, my tendency is to never complete my project and keep on trying to improve. To solve this problem, we focus on delivering daily builds of software to our clients.

Follow Standards to Avoid Re-work

Many young engineers are confused by a healthy tension that exists between individual creative freedom and following team standards. With the pace of business changing, many industries are rapidly adopting Lean techniques in all parts of their business. Lean manufacturing techniques were pioneered by Japanese companies to dominate the automotive industry worldwide. In the context of the software industry, agile methodology is based on an iterative and incremental approach to developing software. The software requirements and solutions evolve through collaboration between self-organizing and cross-functional teams. Agile promotes adaptive planning, evolutionary development, and delivery. Agile encourages rapid and flexible response to change. With agile and lean methodology, individual developers get a lot of creative freedom and are encouraged to solve problems.

In the IT industry, most companies develop common standards that are consistently followed. These standards include how programmers code, how software programs are stored in the source code repository, and how the programs are compiled and quality tools are used. By following programming standards and documenting programs clearly, we as individuals simplify the lives of our co-workers who may be modifying programs or reviewing these programs in the future.

Beyond these team standards, every software developer is encouraged to demonstrate their creativity by developing fast and efficient algorithms and code base.

There are no contradictions here. In some areas, teams want individuals to show their creativity and ingenuity in solving problems. In other areas, we are regimented and follow our team standards to remain organized and efficient.

Guidelines for Meetings

When I left Microsoft Corporation nearly 14 years ago, I decided to create a meeting-free company. I was used to attending several meetings every week that consumed a lot of time. Meetings were very dissatisfying for me and often, because of the number of meetings on my schedule, I got little done.

In a typical company, there are many types of meetings. For example:

+ informational meetings (quarterly update)
+ problem-solving meetings
+ training sessions (Weekly Learning Hour)
+ daily standup meetings for status updates, and
+ meetings with your mentor (one-on-ones)

As a professional, I lead some meetings, while I am a participant in others. And, in many others, I am an observer. My preparation time for each type of meeting differs.

In addition to formal interactions in a meeting, attendees are paying attention to each other's presence (verbal and non-verbal clues). People even watch for small things, including sitting style (leaning back means you are not interested, leaning forward means you are showing interest); clothes; personal grooming (hair and shave); and perfume (I avoid it in air-conditioned, closed offices). Attendees and other managers notice our technical knowledge, confidence, assertiveness, and clarity of thought and communication.

Start and End Meetings on Time

We can learn a lot about the performance of a company based on how meetings are conducted. In most high-performance teams, the meetings start on time. With agile engineering, it is also very important to end meetings on time.

I strive to start meetings when they are scheduled to start, and, more importantly, I try to end meetings when they are supposed to end. Across any company, starting and ending every meeting on time requires discipline and focus. The impact is tremendous. People think, 'I know that this meeting will get over soon, so I better say what I have to say.' Limiting meeting time forces people to be concise and avoid rambling. Otherwise, everyone wastes time.

Limit Meetings to 60 Minutes

I have found that 60 minutes is a very long time for a meeting. Most of us cannot focus beyond 60 minutes. So, by putting an upper limit of an hour to meetings, attendees manage their time more productively. While conducting conference calls (phone meetings), we limit them to 30-minute increments. Unless we are solving a problem or debugging a program, I avoid longer meetings. Longer meetings mean that the participants are not organized and have not thought through the discussion.

Even in the case of technical problem-solving meetings which can be very time consuming, limiting meetings to 90 minutes is useful. With the agile engineering approach now more common than ever, where all team members are required to be present in the meeting (not just the team lead), it is very important for us to utilize meetings properly. Because of the large number of attendees, meeting inefficiency wastes a lot of time for everyone.

In most cases, we can actually discuss a lot of information in 30 minutes. TED talk videos are a great example of how a lot of information can be shared in a short time. TED talks only last for 18 minutes (standard format for a TED presentation).

For example, there is a TED talk video by Dr Atul Gawande of Harvard Medical School that discusses the importance of checklists in avoiding mistakes. In just 18 minutes, Dr Gawande provides a lot of information, with examples and supporting data, in a very compelling manner.

In his talk Dr Gawande discusses two types of mistakes. The first type is an error of ignorance where we make a mistake because we know too little. This type of mistake can be cured through training. The second type is an error where we do not properly use what we already know. Dr Gawande reasons that the second type of mistakes are common because the volume and complexity of knowledge today is very large. For most of us, the volume and complexity of knowledge exceeds our ability to consistently deliver it correctly and safely. By using proper checklists, we can dramatically reduce the instances of the second type of mistakes. Dr Gawande mentions how he helped create a 2-

minute checklist for surgical teams. Eight hospitals, from around the world, reduced their death rates by 47 percent after implementing this checklist. Dr Gawande's talk is very powerful, and it's only 18 minutes long.

Manage Your Boss

BE PART OF THE POLITICS

Is there politics in the workplace? Of course there is. Politics is usually given a bad name, whether we are talking about career politicians or political types in a company. In many companies, I have commonly heard people say, 'Oh, in that company, there is a lot of politics.' What does that mean? *Politics is the way decisions are made by a group of people.*[12] As engineers, we have to take an active part in helping shape discussions by providing technical solutions and being part of the decision-making process. As one of the greatest philosophers Plato stated, 'One of the penalties for refusing to participate in politics is that you end up being governed by your inferiors.'

For me, instead of having a negative mindset, I proactively participate in the decision-making process by offering to provide solutions. Most companies appoint managers based on several factors. Besides the ability to influence decision-making, technical skills are key factors for engineering organizations. Other considerations include a knowledge of the industry, experience in the company, and the ability to lead people.

BE SOLUTION-ORIENTED

Many people come to me with problems. I work with our customers, suppliers, and employees. Their issues range from major strategic problems to technical problems, simple operational challenges, resource limitations, and budgets.

What do I do? I find people who solve these problems for me. They are my 'go to guys'. The reputation of the engineering college they may have attended does not matter to me. The individuals I rely on are resourceful and solution-oriented. Legendary GE CEO Jack Welch pointed out that once you are in the real world—and it doesn't make any difference if you are 22 or 62, starting your first job or your fifth—the way to look great and get ahead is to over-deliver.[13] Successful people proactively anticipate their boss's needs.

As Jack Welch stated, 'If your boss asks you for a report on the outlook for one of your company's products for the next year, you can be sure she already has a solid sense of the answer. So go beyond being the grunt assigned to confirm her hunch. Do the extra legwork and data-crunching to give her something that really expands her thinking—an analysis, for instance, of how the entire industry might play out over the next 3 years. What new companies and products might emerge? What technologies could change the game?'

Similarly, when we go to our customers, we have to solve their problems and be a resource for them.

When clients come to us as a company, what are they looking for? Problems or solutions? Solutions. They're saying, 'If we work with your company's engineers, they should get the work done. They do a good job. They have the technical expertise, they are proactive, they write great software, they do not make mistakes, and they deliver on time. They think from the customer's point of view and understand our challenges.'

When customers have to choose between two companies, they make a decision based on the past performance of each company. The selection has nothing to do with size of the company. Become the 'go to' employee for your boss.

ALIGN YOURSELF WITH YOUR BOSS

All engineers should ask their manager, 'What are your key challenges and how can I make you and the department more successful?'

Don't start by asking, 'When are you going to pay me more?' In most cases, managers do want to pay good performers more, if nothing else then at least for fairness.

For example, one of our senior client managers often tells one of our key clients, 'I want to understand what *your* key challenges are. How can *we* align ourselves to make *you* more successful?' Our client manager does not say, 'How can *you* align *yourselves* with us so that *we* are more successful?'

Often, that client manager has more expertise and experience than our clients in certain areas. Our client manager has more resources at her disposal. But our client manager has to adjust her thinking to make sure the client is successful.

The same idea is true within a company. You have to align yourself with your boss or your department manager. In general, the leader (the boss) gets the credit for the success of the entire department. To be successful yourself, you need to ensure that your boss increases her success. Because if your boss is successful, chances are that the department and the company will be more successful. In return, most bosses give credit to the people who make them successful.

Over my working life, I have not needed a formal title to take a leadership role. Nobody can stop you from improving the company, whether you are a new trainee or a highly-paid engineer.

My first job was as a Mechanical Design Analysis Engineer at Frigidaire. I was working in the Laundry Division, which was responsible for producing about 1 million washing machines and dryers annually. In the major appliance industry, the product life cycle used to be 10 years. Once the design was completed and manufacturing was set up, the company needed to utilize the same design to recover the capital investments in the manufacturing. Once the new design was in production, my challenges were limited as an analyst. Once the department ran out of challenges for me, I needed to find some other way to help our department and be useful.

In the late 1980s, typical of most companies at that time, our engineering department did not have a Local Area Network (LAN). The engineering staff members did not have any personal computers. Our engineering department had a secretary. To circulate any information, she used to prepare a memo using a typewriter. Next, she would attach the memo to the article to be shared with 35 engineering personnel. Then the file would be circulated from one manager to the next and then to the engineers in alphabetical order. We used to initial our name on the memo against our name and physically pass the memo to the next engineer. Sometimes, it would be weeks before a memo reached me.

I realized that companies were installing LANs for file and print sharing. Online forums like CompuServe were enabling e-mail communication and online message boards. Our company, Frigidaire, was owned by a Swedish parent company, AB Electrolux, one of the largest appliance manufacturers at that time. IBM was a key supplier for AB Electrolux. Unlike today, IBM Token ring, AppleTalk, and Ethernet were three competing standards. Ethernet was promoted by every other computer supplier. Since Electrolux's policy department valued IBM direction, we elected to install an IBM Token ring network.

I worked with my manager to help set up cabling for a LAN, networked file share, and shared laser printers. We brought in IBM PS/2 PCs so that we could create documents and review drawings on our IBM PCs. I was able to identify the gaps in our company in relation to the external industry. I helped improve our engineering processes and the environment.

Even the most respected companies face a dearth of qualified candidates to fill senior most positions. One recent example is Infosys. Despite having 200,000 employees and a history of over 32 years, they could not find a leader internally. After many years of uneven performance, Infosys had to bring back Narayana Murthy from his retirement to take over as Chairman again. If there is a gap at the senior-most level, there are an even larger number of gaps at the vice-president level in most companies. Do we think that there is a shortage of engineers at Infosys? No. They have a shortage of CEOs and other senior managers.

The same shortage exists across all industries and in many companies. If you aspire to be a manager in a company, there are ample opportunities to advance yourself in any company. For me, however, to advance, I had to start thinking and delivering like a manager before I was a manager. Many people think, 'I will be an average engineer doing average work. However, when I become a manager, I will do outstanding work!' Typically in most companies, average performers do not get promoted.

Many of us think, 'I would like to get more money.' We all would like to make more money, there's no doubt about that. Most companies don't mind paying more money to high performers. As I explained above, most companies have a shortage of outstanding performers. But, in order for us to be paid more, we have to do outstanding work every day. Many of us want to be paid more for average performance. We have to become more knowledgeable than everyone else in the industry. We have to work harder than everyone else in the industry. We must endeavour to become the most skilled person in the industry.

Work with the IT Team

In most companies, employees are generally dissatisfied with their Information Technology (IT) department. Why? Because they don't understand how the IT department functions.

As part of the support team, a typical IT team balances competing priorities. Computers run by the IT department help deliver services produced by the company to customers in a timely manner. At the same time, they have to lower the cost of producing goods and services, and increase employee productivity. IT departments are tasked with maintaining data security, facilities, and equipment. Employee and customer privacy has become a huge concern worldwide and, ultimately, IT systems help maintain privacy.

All of the systems that IT is responsible for can cause inconvenience for employees. Morale can be affected as employees try to get their work done or access company resources. But the people in the IT department have to keep the systems working that help all employees, while maintaining a positive attitude and providing great customer service.

To complicate things further, technology is always changing. A new version of Internet Explorer is introduced, and suddenly what was working yesterday is no longer working. Employees expect to bring their own smartphones and use company Internet Wi-Fi infrastructure for personal use. These extra devices further burden and complicate the company IT infrastructure and create security challenges.

Most IT departments enforce company policies that are decided centrally based on years of experience and industry best practices. Somewhere in the headquarters, a policy is decided. Then the branch offices or divisions implement these policies in a decentralized manner. The IT person who helps you doesn't decide the centralized policy. Chances are that he or she cannot change the policy. He has to comply with it. You may not agree with the centralized policy, but that's still the policy.

I have found it useful to work with the IT team to understand their challenges and constraints. Once I understand their limitations, I am able to align myself to ensure we are able to get results.

For example, many employees may say, 'Look, I don't need passwords. Why do we need passwords?' Another version is, 'Why do passwords expire every 30 days? My password should never expire.' An

IT support engineer cannot make a decision about changing passwords. Regularly changing passwords is a good IT security practice and is a centralized policy decision.

As a member of our engineering team, I know we frequently need extra software or specialized hardware. So if I tell the IT team in advance, they are able to take care of the matter without creating an emergency for them or for me. I have found it useful to be proactive in informing them of my needs ahead of time. Just because a request is urgent from my point of view, it is not necessarily an emergency for the IT department. They realize that for a lot of engineers, everything is an urgent issue and they may ignore even genuinely urgent requests.

With shrinking IT staffs in most companies, the IT department has to prioritize and decide what is and is not an emergency. Regardless, the IT department is never fast enough for most people.

I try to remember that the IT department has a very challenging role. IT teams are staffed with good people like you and me. Everyone has good intentions; they are trying to solve the same problem, and they have the same goal that we do.

On the other hand, if you are part of an IT department, you can still make a difference even though you don't directly decide the company policies you are enforcing. Successful IT people put in the extra effort to try and understand the rationale behind the policies. They effectively explain the rationale to the end-users. End-users appreciate and are more willing to comply with policies whose intent they understand rather than being bluntly told, 'This is the policy.'

Successful IT team members also take the time to pass on valuable feedback from end users to their managers. It's great to discover when a goal can be achieved through a different procedure, which de-hassles end-users.

Work with the HR Team

The HR team also has a very delicate job of balancing competing priorities. Many employees consider the HR department ineffective and not in touch with the core business of the company. A typical HR department has to balance:

- needs of the business to improve productivity and lower costs
- employee morale
- fairness (equality across employees and across teams)
- customer service

HR team deliverables consist of:

- operations (onboarding new employees, relieving employees, recruitment, training, regulatory compliance, payroll, reimbursements, organizing morale events)

✦ policies and guidelines (budget, legal)—decided centrally and relatively fixed over time

Most companies do not change policies just because of one instance or one situation. These HR policies change once every few years in response to changes in market conditions or laws. Consequently, employee manuals are generally well written and explain many situations we are likely to face as an employee.

From a fairness perspective, most companies treat all of their employees and customers the same way. This is not necessarily the right thing for everyone. For example, if one employee has bad eyesight, then he or she might benefit from a larger monitor. But a company's policy may be that everybody gets the same size of monitor. The same challenges are there to accommodate gender issues.

Most HR departments work with new graduates to explain company guidelines and policies. HR policies are designed to facilitate company objectives. Many employee situations are very complex, without any obvious answer. One single answer is not always appropriate for everyone. Most companies try to be as consistent as possible when they are working with different team members and different situations.

Because employee situations are so dynamic, mistakes do happen. We have to make sure we understand that we can make a mistake and learn from those mistakes. Just as programmers make mistakes in writing code, the HR department may also make mistakes.[14]

The more we understand the HR department's role and responsibilities, the easier it will be to work with them.

Grounds for Disciplinary Action

In my experience, most companies have very strict policies that call for disciplinary action, generally:

- violating core values of the company
- theft
- sharing confidential information on Facebook, blogs, instant messaging
- misrepresentation
- sexual harassment
- workplace violence
- concealing data resulting in business loss
- viewing and storing pornography or other inappropriate content

Checklist for Managing Work

- Limit use of text messaging, cell phone, Facebook, Twitter, e-mail to few times a day
- Avoid distractions at work
- Schedule 6 months to 1 year in advance
- Be on time to the office
- Track items to closure
- Follow team standards
- Start meetings on time
- End meetings on time
- Go to your boss with solutions, not just problems
- Help your boss with their challenges
- Inform IT department of needs ahead of time
- Read employee manual

4

Manage Personal Effectiveness

*'Genius is 1 percent talent and 99 percent
hard work.'*

—ALBERT EINSTEIN
Winner, Nobel Prize for Physics

I left Kharagpur on May 19, 1986. I had worked
hard to earn my B.Tech. (Honours) degree, and I
made lifelong friends in the process. I paid my final
bills to IIT to ensure that I would receive my degree
certificate. I closed my SBI bank account, and I
cleared my hostel room.

Shishir Kumar Biswas (Shishirda) was the post-
man assigned to RK Residence Hall where I stayed.
Shishirda delivered letters from home and was our
crucial link to the outside world. We looked forward
to collecting mail from him. Shishirda used to sit
outside the hostel common room and distribute
letters to us as we arrived for lunch. In those days,
there was no e-mail and a letter used to take 10 days
to arrive. Some letters got lost in the mail. Phone
calls were impractical and expensive.

One of my seniors at the R.K. Hall told me that Shishirda could smell a letter from a university and tell whether the letter included a scholarship. I remember the day when he handed me the scholarship letter from Iowa State University. Before leaving, I gifted my bicycle to him (as was the norm at my hostel).

As I left R.K. Hall for the 'real world', I thought I knew it all. I was a young, confident, arrogant engineer. In reality, I had very low self-awareness (I did not know what I did not know). I lacked many basic self-management skills, including listening, time management, and discipline.

I had a victim mindset where I blamed others for all the difficulties I faced. Having spent all of my time solving technical problems to arrive at the correct answer, I lacked life skills. From a programmed life at college, now I had to define the structure in my life.

In my work with fresh graduates, many lack the self-awareness and skills to survive in the world where they have to manage their own effectiveness. When new graduates join our company, we work with them to help them increase their self-awareness. This includes identifying their personality, work style, and their emotional intelligence (EQ) level.

Without getting into psychology, we discuss internal and external *Locus of Control*[15] to help them avoid a victim mindset. Only after we learn to stop blaming others do we start looking for solutions.

Individuals with an *internal* locus of control believe that events in their life derive from their own actions. If a person with an internal locus of control does not perform well on an exam, they blame it on their *own* lack of preparation. If they did well on the exam, they would attribute this to *their* ability to study.

When a person with an *external* locus of control does poorly on an exam, they feel that the exam was difficult. If they performed well on the exam, they think that they were lucky or the teacher was lenient.

I remember an employee who was late every day to the office by 20–30 minutes. He would come late and say that, 'The traffic was really bad.' Blaming traffic is an *external* locus of control response. An internal locus of control response is, 'I am late because I did not leave on time.' Yes, occasionally there is a public transportation issue in the city, but in those cases quite a few people will be late to the office and not just one person. We worked with that employee to ensure that he planned for daily traffic and left his house earlier.

Each of the following statements is a different view of the same situation.

TABLE 4.1: TWO VIEWS OF THE SAME SITUATION

External	Internal
The client doesn't understand	I need to explain in a better way
I was late because there was traffic	I need to leave earlier and plan for traffic
The software is not working	I don't know how to use the software
The software requirements are not clear	I have not asked the right questions to clarify the requirements
My subordinate makes too many mistakes	I have not trained my subordinate
I don't have time	I did not prioritize
My alarm did not go off	I did not set my alarm correctly
We do not get the right kind of employees	I am not clear on the job requirements and qualifications
No one told me	I didn't ask

When I left my structured life at IIT, I needed to accelerate my personal growth in several areas. As I entered the workforce and society at large, no structure existed for me beyond the office hours (usually 50 hours per week). I needed to personally organize my support system of housing and food. Setting aside another 56 hours per week for sleep, I still had over 60 hours to use any way I wanted. I could waste these hours or use them productively to advance myself.

Many new graduates have the same opportunity.

Leadership Qualities

Early in my career, I learned that I can lead at any level. My sphere of influence will be smaller depending on my role, but I can always practice leadership. The common thread I've seen with successful people across the industry is that they began practising leadership early. Successful people do not wait for titles to become leaders.

TABLE 4.2: TOP EXPECTATIONS OF LEADERS AT VARIOUS LEVELS

Recent Graduates	Middle Managers	Top Leaders
Hard work	Ability to Motivate Others	Vision
Proactivity	Decisiveness	Ability to Motivate Others
Reliability	Industry Experience	Decisiveness
Intelligence	Networking Ability	Ability to Handle Crisis
Ambition	Delegation	Honesty

Source: Owen, *The Leadership Skills Handbook: 50 Key Skills from 1,000 Leaders*

Over the last few years, I have read a lot of books on management and leadership. Most of the books describe a leader in a particular context. In *The Leadership Skills Handbook,*[16] Jo Owen surveyed 1,000 leaders. The author asked what traits leaders are expected to possess. By reviewing the results, I realized that the expectations are different as we move from entry-level roles to middle management and senior levels.

To progress to middle management, I had to acquire and master additional skills and behaviours. These included acquiring industry knowledge and the abilities to decide and delegate.

I have seen many fresh graduates stumble over these basic expectations. If you focus on these basics, you will stand out from your peer group.

TITLES VARY BY INDUSTRY

As I gained work experience and interacted with customers in many industries, I realized that leadership and titles vary by industry, organization, and individual. Those titles usually are very subjective, and are not consistent across all situations.

For example, the vice president title is used commonly by banks even for mid-level employees. In many banks, that title is held by a department manager. The reasons that banks hand out titles liberally may range from customer expectations— some customers might only be willing to discuss their finances with a senior person—to the need to meet regulatory or legal requirements. Meanwhile, in a company like IBM, the vice president title is given rarely and is usually only given to very senior executives. That person is responsible for managing hundreds, if not thousands of people.

Similarly, a manager of a research-and-development team of PhDs manages very differently than a manager of a customer service department. Both managers are doing similar managerial tasks, but the expectations and the power structure are very different.

Also, I did not realize that I did not need to be the CEO to become a leader. All of us have opportunities to take initiative and improve the performance of our department and our company. As I observed some of the successful people in the industry, I came to learn that they understood and began practising leadership early and consistently in their careers. They did not wait for a formal title to become a leader.

WORK STYLE AND PERSONALITY

Coming from a very technical background, I had not understood work style and personality. Before I could lead others, I had to increase my self-awareness. Many people are 35- or 40-years-old before they know what does and does not work for them. That was certainly the case with me. I am still working to understand myself better so that I can understand others better.

Our personality and work style are huge parts of who we are. The current thinking is that many personality traits appear early in life. These personality traits remain with us throughout our lives.

DISC (Dominance, Influence, Steadiness, and Compliance) and *People Styles at Work*[17] are two simple tools that you can use to understand your work styles better. Many other free tests are available online to help us increase our self-awareness.

Working well with people is a critical managerial skill. As I learned more about managing people, it was useful for me to learn about a person's natural work style. To work well with people very different than me, I need to predict how they are likely to do things. How do they like to be treated? I can then make minor adjustments to my behaviour to adapt to their preferences.

Next, as a manager I can align their roles with their natural strengths and preferred work style. These personality types are not meant to stereotype people; they help people align with jobs they will enjoy more naturally. The more someone enjoys their job, the more successful they will be.

Find the Balance

During my second year as an MBA student at the University of Michigan, businessman and author Stephen Covey conducted a one-day workshop for the students. While discussing his book, *The Seven Habits of Highly Effective People*, he told us with great emotion how many senior executives who hold top positions in leading companies were very unhappy. Outside of work, they had few close relationships. Many did not have a family because they focussed only on their career. Some treated their spouses worse than they would treat a stranger, ignoring small courtesies like holding a door open. Many failed to take care of their health and were very sick.

Nearly 20 years later, as I think about his comments, Covey was asking us to find the balance in four dimensions of our life:

- taking care of ourselves as a person (health, spiritual needs, and stress)
- growing ourselves professionally
- taking care of our families, and
- engaging with our broader community

I had to learn to balance competing needs for resources in all four areas to be happy in the long run. If I lack in one area, I am not effective.

Learn to Learn

When I was in college, I was introduced to five new subjects every semester. I learned a lot. I had to learn these subjects and prove that I had absorbed the information by clearing examinations.

When I joined the industry in the late 1980s, my pace of learning slowed considerably. After I had learned how to do my job, I was not required to read any books to stay employed. We read a few industry magazines every month, primarily to glean competitive information. As engineers, most of us did not have to take any examinations to prove our knowledge. Changes were incremental and most of us resisted change. Many of us did not appreciate learning and mastering new skills or technologies. Many did not even read a single new book in a year. Determined to advance myself, I made an extra effort to visit book stores and find books to read.

> *'The man who does not read good books has no advantage over the man who can't read them.'*
>
> —MARK TWAIN
> Celebrated American author

With the advent of the Internet, the pace of change in most industries became very fast. Learning has become easier since access to information, book catalogs, and lectures are readily available. Now, I order several books from Amazon each week to stay up-to-date and improve my skills. Instead of watching TV or gossiping, I read to improve my knowledge.

At MAQ Software, we require our engineering team members to improve their technical skills every year. We take exams to *certify* our learning. We learn how to easily learn new technologies faster than our competition.

To learn about a new area, I start by reading college textbooks used for the subject. For IT engineers, I ask them to review data structures and databases textbooks. Most textbooks include the theory and a survey of recent advances in that field.

If I do not understand basic concepts, I cannot apply them correctly. Only after completing a review of textbooks do I read documents and training manuals for tools (e.g., Visual Studio and SQL Server).

I also find and ask the experts in the company for their reading recommendations. I also search Amazon.com for bestselling books (crowdsourcing) and popular Internet blogs about the technology I am working on.

As I reflect on the leaders who survived the bad economic cycles, all of them were habitual learners. I have yet to find an exception to this rule.

LEARN ANY WAY YOU CAN

Learning also takes place outside of classrooms and books. As a student, I learned from my professors. However, I also learned through work projects. When I was in Michigan, I had already earned a Master's degree and had an undergraduate degree from IIT. Similar to many MBA students today, I had worked for several years before joining the MBA program.

At that time, I thought I wanted to be in finance, so I applied for a part-time student job posted in my department by a finance professor. The job offered student pay, which wasn't very much, and involved reading data from microfiche and entering it into an Excel file.

I went to the professor and said, 'I would like to apply for this job.'

She said, 'This is a data entry job. You already have a Master's degree along with industry experience. Do you really want this job?'

I said, 'Yes.'

She replied, 'Do you realize that it's tedious? You'll have to go to the library, find the microfiche for companies, enter the data into Excel, and give it to me every week.'

I said, 'Yes, I want the job.'

What was the project? She was compiling information about initial public offerings (IPOs) and the shareholding patterns of insiders. The data involved information on how a company's stock rises after its IPO. She was studying the correlation between stock ownership and performance.

My job was not to study the correlation. My job was entering data. However, while I was entering the information from the microfiche, I learned a lot about how businesses are formed. I learned about the people who make the decisions on forming a business and what their qualifications were. To someone else this might just have been a data entry job. To me, it was a learning opportunity.

In my second year at the University of Michigan, Ann Arbor, I took a job that helped me get my position at Microsoft. I worked part-time for the university's Intellectual Properties Office, which was responsible for licensing technology developed by the university. The Intellectual Properties Office took the technology that was developed at the university and licensed it to companies.

Every year, the department manager hired a few MBA students to market the technologies developed at the university. My role was to contact companies to see if they had any interest in licensing the technology developed at the University of Michigan. The department manager clarified to me that the job did not pay a lot. However, I wanted an opportunity to learn and gain experience. Since all my savings were exhausted, I could also use the pay and not add to my student loans.

Recognizing my mechanical engineering background, the department manager assigned me to work with a young assistant professor of Mechanical Engineering at the University of Michigan.

The professor had developed software that simulated vehicle dynamics on a PC. He thought that I was a marketing expert and asked me about go-to-market plans for his software technology. I had to think about the four Ps of marketing. I had to understand the product features, develop a pricing proposal, promote the product, and know its distribution. Once I had developed a list of potential buyers, I compiled a list of 10 companies we could license the software to. I phoned (cold called) companies, which was something I had never done before. The next year, when Microsoft was looking for product marketing managers, I was able to fluently discuss the marketing challenges I had faced. My experience at the Intellectual Properties Office made me a strong candidate.

At the University of Michigan, we also had opportunities to volunteer our time with local non-profits. I worked with a non-profit that helps mentally challenged people lead normal lives. Typical of most non-profits, the local organization lacked sufficient funds and needed marketing help. My effectiveness in raising funds turned out to be limited. I learned that it is really difficult to raise money for non-profits.

For me, campus jobs were a great way to gain knowledge and acquire skills in different areas. While some of these student jobs did not pay well in relation to my tuition, I did develop skills that were useful later.

Many of our key leaders originally started working as test engineers. One of our key managers started as a temporary data entry person. He started compiling data about the companies from the Internet. When the data entry project finished, many of his colleagues left. However, instead of leaving, he sought out new assignments within the company. He offered to help with accounting and administration. He knew a lot about computer hardware and started helping. Eventually, he took over the IT department. He rose through the ranks rapidly despite starting at a very low level temporary job role. In my experience, it is possible to develop skills and grow ourselves in any area.

LEARNING HOUR

Most professionals in the software industry spend between 45 and 55 hours per week at work. I encourage everyone to dedicate just 1 hour to learning a new skill or improving their knowledge of the software. Even on an informal basis, we can create a study group of 7–10 people. We can take turns discussing a new topic or a new development in the industry. I have seen many successful professionals create a study group to clear a specific industry certification (e.g., Agile PMP).

Yes, we have a lot of work pressure and deadlines every week. We are busy. However, by spending just 1 hour every week in Learning Hour (2 percent of our time), we ensure that the other 98 percent of our time goes well. As Stephen Covey mentioned, 'Sharpen the Saw'[18] is one of the seven habits of highly effective people. Over the years, our company has found it very useful to set aside just 1 hour every week to learn.

Ask for Help

When I interact with new graduates, I find that they frequently do not ask for help. Reasons vary by individual, from lack of self-confidence and self-image to a busy workplace.

At work, almost any problem or challenge we face has been handled by someone else within the company. We encourage everyone to ask for help. As a manager, I realize that a new engineer may not know everything. However, most supervisors in our company do not have time to answer the same question again. Once we point the way, we expect our engineers to learn.

As the legendary Jack Welch mentioned in his *Business Week* column,[19] next time you have a question, get up from your chair. Do not send an e-mail. Instead, walk to the person down the hall and talk to them in person. Relationships are built better in person. If we get to know our colleagues, help is easier. We are so addicted to electronic communication through Facebook, Twitter, Skype, and e-mail that we are using these even as we talk to each other and eat lunch.

Earn your Pay

Most companies earn net profit margins of less than 10 percent, if they report a profit at all. When I worked for Frigidaire, John Patrou, our Division President, used to be concerned about ensuring just 6 percent net profit. I admire every company that earns a profit. Despite our best efforts, in some years our division did not earn any profit. Still, we were investing in personal computers to improve our efficiency.

As an engineer, I used to work with our Information Technology (MIS) group to computerize our engineering department. We used to buy IBM PS/2 computers for our engineering team. Occasionally, IBM would run promotions that included a mail-in rebate of $200 per personal computer. Sending in the rebate required filling out the IBM rebate form, providing a sales receipt, and providing a proof of purchase from the IBM PS/2 carton. Because of inefficiencies, many companies do not claim simple mail-in rebates.

I used to diligently send in for the $200 rebate every time. As I found other departments, including Purchasing, that were installing PCs, I went ahead and helped claim additional rebates. My manager appreciated that I proactively informed concerned departments to help reduce expenditures in a very tough economic climate. No one would have noticed or complained if I had not claimed rebates. I claimed the rebates because I wanted to help my company.

As an employee, I always looked out for the best interest of my employer. I was always a 'company man' and put the company's interest before my personal interest. I was more frugal with my employer's money than I was with my own. If your company is doing well, eventually you will also do well.

Over the years, I got to know one of my IIT juniors well. He had left a large IT services provider to join a mid-size company in India. His company sent 2 project managers and 10 engineers to work with a Fortune 500 client. He was one of the 2 project managers working from the client's location.

In just a few months, my IIT friend (the first project manager) made a difference on the client's project. He was very thoughtful and methodical. He was well liked. After a few months, the project was running smoothly and the environment was stable.

The second project manager (a non-IIT graduate) was also very skilled. His team also completed their work and performed well. As a consultant, the second project manager kept track of the key people in the Fortune 500 client organization. The second project manager sought out new project opportunities. Many suppliers were competing for the same project work from the Fortune 500 client. The second project manager helped his sales team understand the internal politics and competitive dynamics at the Fortune 500 company. He pro-actively spent a few hours every month meeting with key decision makers. He educated them about his company's expertise. As a result of his efforts, the second project manager increased sales in addition to completing his project management work.

The director of his company in India asked the first project manager to expand his role, to seek new projects opportunistically with the Fortune 500 client. My IIT friend refused. As a senior project manager, my IIT friend reasoned that he should not be asked to sell or help facilitate sales. Instead he mentioned that since his project was going well, he should be paid more.

When the company evaluated the two project managers for promotion, they did not promote my IIT friend. Instead, the company promoted the second project manager since he took a larger view for the organization. He took ownership of growing the business with their Fortune 500 client. My IIT friend was bitter and felt victimized. He ended up leaving his employer and was unemployed for several months.

As I work with many consultants, I find that they take a narrow view of their job role. Many consultants do a great job technically, but they do not help their organization expand their business with clients.

In my last job at Microsoft Corporation, I served as a product marketing manager for Microsoft Exchange, a messaging and collaboration server. Exchange had low market share and IBM Lotus Notes was the market leader. I used to visit many computer industry tradeshows. During tradeshows, product managers like me used to demonstrate Exchange software product functionality at a booth (booth duty). When I was off my booth duty, I took time to visit the Lotus Notes booth. I filled out postcards at Lotus' booth that added me to their prospective customer database. As a result, I regularly received Lotus Notes product information and promotional offers from IBM by mail.

While I was working as a Microsoft product manager, I received an invitation from IBM to attend a half-day Lotus Notes seminar. I attended the seminar to increase my knowledge of the competing product and IBM. After the seminar, I sent a short e-mail report to our extended marketing team about the Lotus Notes product features and market positioning. How many people attended? What product demonstration was done? If IBM discussed my product, Exchange, how did they position it?

Forty-seven people attended the IBM seminar that day. At the end, IBM did a drawing for an IBM ThinkPad laptop. As luck would have it, I won the laptop lottery. A few weeks later, I received the laptop from IBM. Since I already had a laptop, I sold the laptop on eBay. Then I donated the money from the sale to a school in India. I felt really good about being able to help a school in rural India—a feeling I would not have gotten if I had not stretched myself.

Attending the IBM seminar was not part of my job description, nor was sending a report about the competition. In fact, very few employees do the extra due diligence to learn about their company's competitive landscape.

Not everyone at our company has a client-facing role. Not everyone has to take a broader view of their job role in the same way. However, by giving three very different examples in very different job roles and situations, I showed that all of us can save money for the company or grow sales. We can help bring in our own salary.

I am frequently asked, 'I am only a junior engineer. How can I help?' So how do some entry-level engineers expand their view of their own job role? Here are a few practices I have seen from the resourceful people in our company:

    ✦ Refer qualified job candidates to the company. Every company needs great people. Even though I never worked formally in the HR department,

I recruited several people for my past employer. Some of my referrals are doing very well even though I have left

+ Share cost-saving ideas from other friends from other industries (not just the IT industry)

+ Help the recruitment team connect with your campus professors

+ Deliver campus presentations as an alumni to your college. With Skype and Google Hangout, we do not have to leave our desk to give a presentation

+ *Like* our own employer page on Facebook, Twitter, and LinkedIn. Many employers advertise on Facebook to increase Likes. I do my part and *Like* all of our clients and key suppliers on their Facebook pages. *Liking* a company page on Facebook does not cost me anything. Through my *Likes*, I promote our key clients and key suppliers. I show my gratitude without much effort

Prioritize

When I was in college, all classes had equal importance to me. All of my classes gave me three credits, and I had to take five classes (15 credits) every semester to graduate.

Unlike in university classes, in life and in business not everything is equal. Not all e-mail messages are equally important; neither are all people, all phone calls, or all meetings. In our context, work hierarchy goes from client to manager to co-worker to subordinate.

When I receive a phone call from a client, I drop everything and attend to that call. Chances are that the client has something urgent, they are pressed for time, or they need something delivered. I change my priorities according to the client's needs. Similarly, phone calls from managers to subordinates take priority over casual social chats.

Often during my conversations with new engineers, if their cell phone rings, they interrupt our discussion and take the personal call. But I was the priority; I was talking to the engineer before the call came in. Organizational hierarchy aside, even if we handle phone calls only on first-come, first-served, I should have had priority.

In my career, I took up assignments others were not willing to take on. Most of us want to do what everybody else is doing. The problem with that approach is that if you do what everyone else is doing, you remain average. In order to go above average, I had to find and do things that very few people were willing to do.

Many of us have friends who are just as intelligent as we are, but who did not get into engineering college. Why? Because they were unwilling to study as much we were. The same books, same teachers, and same material were available to them, but we took the time to study with interest. Again, to be above average, we have to do things others are not willing to do.

I try to learn something new every day. I rely on books and the Internet. In the past, I would not have been able to hear a noteworthy speaker unless I went to a conference where that speaker was featured. Now, because the Internet is the great equalizer, that same speaker and conference are available to me with at least 90 percent effectiveness. Time zone and location are no longer disadvantages. I can get most of a speaker's message without spending even 1 percent of the effort I used to. Furthermore, many of these educational resources are free.

I spend about 7 hours every week in my car. For 3 out of those 7 hours, I listen to educational podcasts and technical talks on CDs. Instead of complaining about traffic, I utilize my time to learn. Periodically, I repeat the same CD and every time I listen to it, I learn something new. They are great sources of new ideas and knowledge for me.

All of us work differently. I need focussed time to be fully productive. I have realized that I am slow and it takes longer for me to finish projects. For nearly 25 years, I have gone to the office regularly on weekends for several hours. During those hours, when others are not distracting me, I finish many of my individual work items. On a typical Monday morning, my co-workers have a lot of new e-mail from me because I'm thinking and sending e-mail over the weekend. I am compiling information and reviewing work issues to see how we can contribute that information to grow the company.

I have one simple technique. I complete easy items first. While I am doing the easy things, I am also thinking in the background about the more complex things I have to do. I'm learning the context of difficult problems and alternate approaches. I'm getting practice for the more complicated items.[20]

AVOID PEER PRESSURE

'Avoid peer pressure' is the *only* advice I offered to my son when he was entering high school. We adopt bad behaviours faster than we learn good behaviours from our friends. According to a June 2013 article in *The Wall Street Journal*, scientists suggest that teens are more vulnerable to peer pressure than adults.[21] Teens get greater pleasure from behaviours they experience as rewarding. Teens find being liked by other people as very gratifying.

Though peer pressure affects all kids, risky, 'bad' behaviours (drinking alcohol, speeding) tend to be associated with being popular. Kids who are less popular, or who have low self-esteem, are more easily influenced by peers. For the good behaviours, such as doing well in studies, peer influence is not as effective.

Most of us fall for peer pressure. While 'crowd-sourcing' has advantages when making purchases, I've found that most people do what everybody else is doing. As a result, we end up being average. We apply for a particular job just because everybody else is applying for it. We accept jobs that are popular.

For instance, 5 years ago, the retail industry was very hot in India. Everybody wanted to be in the retail industry because that was the industry that was hiring. When I looked at the salaries and the job profiles in the retail industry I thought, *This is unsustainable. Those companies do not have the profit margins or customers to justify their level of expenditures.* Salaries fell. The same thing happened in the airline industry. Good times do not last forever.

When choosing careers, I find it useful to study the economics of the entire industry. Some industries are capital intensive (e.g., Intel manufacturing plants and Ford plants) while others are knowledge-worker oriented (e.g., Infosys, Apollo Hospitals). In some industries, knowledge-work and innovation is valued more than capital investments. When I had a choice, I chose to be in sectors where I could utilize my skills to the fullest. I joined the company and the industry where I would be challenged.

Over the years, I have worked hard to avoid peer pressure. I avoided peer pressure to spend money on the latest cars, expensive designer clothes, and trendy restaurants or bars. I had the courage to walk away if I was not comfortable with a situation. If it did not feel right, I declined the invitation or left early despite social pressure.

Manage Leaves

In the world of management, there are two kinds of leaves: planned and unplanned leaves. Most employers in India offer over 4 weeks (20 days) of paid earned leaves, including sick days, Founder's Day, and casual leaves. In addition, many employers offer paid national and regional holidays.

While it is true that you have earned the right to utilize your leaves, unplanned leaves are disruptive for your team and customers. If you plan your leaves in advance, the team can organize for your absence. Unplanned absences by members in a fast-paced team in a fast-moving industry cause havoc. If you take many unplanned leaves (for instance, you are absent every second week), chances are you will not progress in the company. If I cannot count on someone to be present on a regular basis, I think twice about assigning critical work to that person.

As I progressed in my career, I could not even plan to take all of my earned leaves as the pace of business and competition increased. My experience is similar to the experience of many other senior managers across different industries. These senior managers are in touch with their offices regardless of their time zone. I realized that if I want to grow faster than my colleagues, I can't be out of the office for 5 weeks in a year.

I advise everyone at our company to plan 2 weeks in a year for a planned vacation to recharge their energy, and attend weddings and social events. Plan to take one unplanned leave every month for health or family emergencies. Save a few days every year for personal emergencies, which I hope you never have to take.

PLAN LEAVES 3–6 MONTHS IN ADVANCE

One of the reasons great institutions like IIT are so successful is because they publish their academic calendar in advance for the whole year. Once published, the calendar does not change. As a result, thousands of students can plan their travel, their holidays, and family events. In my final year at IIT Kharagpur, the mess workers' union was in a labour dispute with the IIT administration. Since Kharagpur was a small town, all students ate at the hostel dining facility run by the mess workers. To press for their demands, the mess workers decided to go on a strike during the final semester exams in April 1986. A mess worker's strike generally crippled the institute since most of the students would spend inordinate time finding food or leave for home. Exams and the IIT schedule would have been delayed. Russi Mody, the then Chairman of the IIT Kharagpur Board of Governors, decided to stay with the examination schedule for the final year students. Russi Mody brought in food suppliers from Jamshedpur to supply boxed lunches during exams. This a great example of the IIT system staying with their calendar.

Almost all universities publish their calendar in advance. Unfortunately, many universities in India do not stick to their calendar and regularly delay their exams.

Even at IIT Kharagpur, some events like Convocation were not fixed. They changed every year, probably to accommodate the commencement speaker. Many graduates like me could not attend their convocation due to last-minute scheduling by the university (as opposed to the weekend after the final examinations at US universities).

The practice of publishing an annual calendar is common across all great systems, including companies, religions, and even countries. Just imagine the chaos if India's Independence Day changed every year.

When I am planning my year, I try to see how I can align myself with the key learning opportunities at the company. Most companies do not change their training program just because a few people cannot attend. Just like a festival date, our training dates do not change. By reviewing the calendar, we choose whether we want to learn and grow by attending the training events.

By combining national holidays and personal leaves, I am able to align my other meetings and interests with those travel dates. Travelling is much easier and less expensive if I plan for it.

Manage Travel

Some of us work in large cities and have family members in neighbouring towns. We find that many engineers go to their hometown for the weekend—every weekend. Then, they take the overnight bus and try to rush into the office Monday morning at 11 am.

If they want to be in a position of seniority, they will not be able to sustain that exercise over time.

Missing sleep due to travel on a weekly basis puts a lot of stress on the human body. For most people who I have seen try do that, their health suffered, which affected their performance at work.

By planning ahead to utilize 3-day weekends, many engineers can easily spend 2 full days at their hometown with their family and friends. By travelling on Friday night and reaching home in the early hours of Saturday, they can spend their entire Saturday and Sunday with family/friends. By returning to their city of work on Monday evening, engineers can show up for work on Tuesday refreshed and well rested.

In planning our company calendar, we maximize 3-day weekend opportunities. Our calendar is similar to the US calendar, with many holidays on Mondays (e.g., Memorial Day, Labour Day).

For example, twice a year, I catch the Lucknow Mail leaving New Delhi Railway station at 10 pm and reaching my hometown of Shahjahanpur by 4.20 am. I reverse my journey on Sunday night, leaving Shahjahanpur around midnight by Delhi Mail to reach Delhi by 7 am. In the last 14 years, I have travelled to my hometown over 25 times from New Delhi, every time by train. For many, travelling by car is more flexible and enjoyable. Despite the inconvenient timing and usual train delays, I take the train every time. I am improving my odds of being safe since I find trains safer compared to travelling by car.

Earlier in my life, I used to wait at home and then rush to the train station or airport at the last minute. Now, trains and airlines have become more punctual and organized. If I am late, I miss the train or flight.

Now, I avoid last-minute excitement (stress) rushing to catch the train or flight. Invariably, traffic is worse the day I am running late. The taxi driver has to stop to fill petrol in the taxi. Due to rushing, the driver is also stressed and is likely to make mistakes. He may hit someone or take a wrong turn causing further delay. When I have extra time, I hardly notice these annoyances. Now, I tell my family members that I get stressed if I am late to the airport. I politely but firmly mention that I would like to leave early.

Waiting at the airport is boring for me. However, I prefer to avoid stress and get to the airport early. I leave from home half an hour earlier than necessary.

I try to relax and get rest on the weekend. Besides sleep, I complete my errands and personal work, catch up on my phone calls, and organize myself for the upcoming week. Senior managers in most companies, including me, use Sunday evening to catch up on their work and get organized for Monday. I avoid social dinners and movie outings on Sunday evening to ensure that I am able to sleep early. I am fully rested for the coming week.

Improve English-Language Skills

Over the years, I have interviewed and worked with many engineers in India. Despite their technical knowledge and hard work, many could not reach their full potential because of their poor English vocabulary and grammar. We could not promote many of them to bigger roles because they could not write or speak grammatically correct English. Some of them have good communication skills in their native language. However, English is a challenge.

When evaluating people, I do my best not to confuse command of English with intelligence and technical ability. Still, when I encounter someone with a poor command of the English language, it affects my opinion of that person.

In the late 1970s, as I was growing up in Shahjahanpur, UP, we had only one English-medium school (run by an American missionary). It was a long distance from our house. Since the rickshaw system was unreliable and there were no school buses, I studied at a nearby local Government Intermediate College (GIC) where classes were conducted in Hindi. I could cycle to school with my younger brothers.

In the early 1980s, the IIT Joint Entrance Examination (JEE) was only held in English. I had excellent Physics and Chemistry books but they were written in Hindi. I needed to improve my English to clear the IIT JEE. There were many common English words that I did not know how to pronounce. To improve, I listened to the news on All India Radio in Hindi at 8.40 pm. At 9 pm, the same news was repeated in English, which helped me increase my English vocabulary and learn pronunciation.

When I was growing up, Indira Gandhi had imposed a state of emergency in 1975 for nearly 2 years. All of the newspapers and radio stations were censored. To get real news, one of our family friends mentioned the radio frequency (I think 213 on a single band radio) British Broadcasting Corporation (BBC) used to broadcast world news. BBC World News covered India every day at 8.10 pm in English. To account for electricity shortages, most homes had a battery-powered portable radio. Using this device, we used to tune in to BBC's radio station to hear uncensored news about India. BBC World News became another source of spoken English for me.

With improvements in English TV programming, it is possible to turn on close captioning (screen text) so that we can follow unfamiliar words.

Typical of the Hindi belt, bookshops in my area did not have any books in English. In the pre-Internet days, there was no book catalog, so I could not select books in English to buy. We did have the *Hindustan Times* newspaper and an Oxford dictionary, which helped me improve my English. But I still had more to learn as I discovered later.

When I joined the Master's in engineering program at Iowa State University, I was a Teaching Assistant (TA) assigned to teach Statics 274 to 2nd year engineering students. As part of the admissions process, I had cleared required examinations, including the GRE and TOEFL. To improve teaching, Iowa State University had adopted a new policy requiring all TAs to go through a test to evaluate their English speaking skills. Having studied at IIT for many years in English, I was fairly confident of clearing the qualifying examination. However, when the results came, I was the only TA from India who did not clear the examination. Iowa State University strongly recommended that I take a remedial class with a speech instructor to help me improve my spoken English. That was the requirement to keep my TA job, which paid my tuition and a monthly stipend.

The test results were a blow to my self-esteem. Initially, I refused to accept the results as fair. I let my teacher know that I should not be in the class. Despite my resentment, she was kind enough to let me continue. She worked really hard to help me improve my spoken English. In hindsight, I am grateful to her.

I suffered from what researchers call *superiority bias* or a *sense of relative superiority*. Unskilled individuals mistakenly rate their ability much higher than average.

In one study, Cornell researchers tested university students on their grammar skills. The bottom 25 percent of the students scored in the 10th percentile. Before hearing their low scores, they estimated their grammar ability and performance on the test to be in the 67th and 61st percentiles respectively.[22] Follow up studies showed that the students improved their ability to estimate their rank after minimal tutoring in the skills they had previously lacked. They improved their ability to estimate regardless of their negligible improvement in actual skills.

Since communication is one of the biggest challenges most companies face, I teach a written English workshop for our engineers every 6 months. We have repeated the same workshop twice a year for the past 10 years. In the workshop, participants review our e-mail messages to improve them for context, grammar, punctuation, conciseness, and clarity. By teaching this workshop, I refresh my own skills and am reminded of my own mistakes. Our supervisors who help lead the workshops also benefit by improving their own skills and those of their team members.

Instead of blaming the school system or our teachers, we can take action to improve our English every day. Those of you who studied in Hindi-medium schools like me may need to try harder. Practice makes perfect, and developing language skills is no exception.

At our company, we encourage engineers to practice speaking in English with colleagues at work, instead of using their native language. This affords them the opportunities to make mistakes in a safe environment, without any embarrassment, and get constructive feedback from colleagues.

There's nothing wrong with deliberate practice to improve our communication skills. In many companies, informal groups like Toastmaster's Club help members improve their presentations.

To help improve English skills, we work with our engineers to assess their vocabulary, grammar, and comprehension. Once we share the test results, many engineers become aware of their own deficiency and take steps to improve their English. For most adults, learning a language takes many years and there is no quick fix.

Many free websites are available to help us improve our English. Even if we spend just 10 minutes per day consistently, we can significantly improve our vocabulary and grammar. Even now, I work to improve my English and communication skills.

I've listed several words non-native English speakers commonly misuse in Appendix-D. There's also a table showing some common poor translations of Hindi to English.

Behave Properly in the Cafeteria

People judge us by the way we present ourselves. As we progress in our career, we will eat with senior managers or customers, and we need to know how to conduct ourselves professionally.

I always wash my hands before and after I eat. It's a matter of basic health and cleanliness. Hand-washing prevents me from getting sick and from spreading germs.

I don't eat with my fingers. I use the utensils provided. It's more professional and less distracting.

When eating with senior managers, I order dishes that are not messy. Fried chicken or ribs get my hands and clothes dirty. It is hard to take anyone with curry sauce smeared across their face seriously.

It's important to understand the pace of lunch. Sometimes it's better to order a readymade meal than a dish that takes a while to cook. It's also considered basic courtesy to wait until everyone at the table has their food before anyone begins eating.

Wear Proper Clothing

Over the last 25 years, I have worked in over 40 office spaces. These offices ranged from a desk in a windowless basement, a shared desk available part time only, and cubicles, to an office with a window. Regardless of the location and time of year, I, along with my co-workers, faced a common problem: our office was either too hot or too cold for some people. Some of us are used to warm weather and need a warmer office; some of us are used to colder weather and feel more comfortable with lower temperatures.

To mitigate this problem while setting up our newest facility in Hyderabad, we decided to triple the temperature sensors that architects normally recommend to solve the temperature problem. However, despite our best efforts, our office is still too hot or too cold for some. The final answer is simple: I wear multiple layers of clothing (sweater or shawls) to adjust to the office temperature.

Even though we may not have customer meetings on a regular basis, we expect everyone to dress professionally with clean clothes. We also encourage our employees to have a pair of semi-formal clothes and formal leather shoes for presentations and client visits.

We also ask everyone to dress conservatively to look professional.

I *always* wear shoes and avoid wearing loose sandals or slippers. Besides appearing more professional, I avoid injuries and accidents due to broken glass and nails present on the road. I have seen many people who could have avoided injury if they had worn shoes.

Manage Your Friends and Family

As I studied people who were successful and organized, I saw that they helped establish the expectations of people in their lives. Those successful families took time to educate their friends and relatives.

In my own situation, my parents know that during work hours, I am busy. They do not phone me at work. They know I am available from 7 am to 8 am, and then after 7 pm. In fact, I've gone to the next step and scheduled a call with them every Saturday morning.

Earlier this year, I moved to Skype video for most calls with my family. That way, when I am spending 30 minutes with them, we are directing our full attention at one another. Otherwise, they are watching TV and talking to me at the same time.

Sometimes when I receive a phone call, I am in front of a computer with e-mail. Or, I may be busy and in a business meeting or with friends. I recognize that I cannot and do not need to answer every phone call immediately. I can and do choose to return the call at a different time. Most successful people I know follow this approach.

Next, when I do return a phone call, I do not multitask. I have a much more engaged and meaningful conversation in a shorter time. Most young professionals do not recognize this pattern of behaviour.

Show Gratitude

I am thankful to all my teachers, supervisors, employers, and clients. All of them gave me opportunities that helped me grow personally and professionally. In addition, many friends, co-workers, relatives, and family members helped me become successful in ways never mentioned to me.

Earlier in my life, I used to hold grudges and criticize people for past wrongs. As I matured, I realized that I needed to learn to forgive. Now I think of these incidents as learning opportunities. Otherwise, I am responsible for holding myself back.

With a sincere 'thank you' mindset, I am able to positively focus on my work and move forward.

Checklist for Managing Personal Effectiveness

❖ Read two industry-related books per month

❖ Read industry magazines

❖ Watch industry lectures

❖ Plan leaves 6 months in advance

❖ Attend company events

❖ Avoid busy traffic times

❖ Practice English daily for 10 minutes—both verbal and written

❖ Use correct eating utensils

❖ Dress conservatively

❖ Dress for the weather

❖ Always wear shoes

❖ Own a set of formal clothes

❖ Keep a 'thank you' mindset

5

Manage Health and Money

'There is this difference between the two temporal blessings—health and money; money is the most envied, but the least enjoyed; health is the most enjoyed, but the least envied; and this superiority of the latter is still more obvious when we reflect.'

—CHARLES CALEB COLTON
English cleric and writer

As I think about long-term success, my own health and personal finances matter. I have seen very successful people suffer because they did not take care of their health. Similarly, without disciplined use of our income over a long time, it is impossible to gain financial independence.

Health

'Take care of your body. It's the only place you have to live.'

—JIM ROHN
Self-made American millionaire and personal-development coach

Until about 3 years ago, I was spending time on pretty much everything else except my health. I was very focussed on being busy. Health was not one of my priorities. I took more interest and knew more about my cell phone than my own body. As a result, my performance suffered. I was unhappy. I could not focus.

Most companies in India have professionals in their early 30s and 40s who are overweight due to bad diet and lack of exercise. We also have a lot of misinformation about our traditional diet. Earlier this year, the *New York Times*[23] ran an article mentioning that our older relatives keep telling us that desi ghee is good, paneer is great, and that dal is entirely protein. All of this is wrong.

Many new websites, mobile applications, and books now cover Indian food and help us learn more. I thought that I was very active until I started tracking my calories using a Body Media Fit band. I wear it around my arm. Only with tracking did I realize that I was not as active as I thought. There are many Android applications that help track our activity and food. HealthifyMe, a company based in Bangalore, offers an Android application for tracking calories in Indian food.

I have a medical checkup every year, even if I am not sick. Annual medical checkups over the years saved my life. With age, eating fried foods and sugary sweets, I had developed heart disease (due to high cholesterol). I was overweight. Worse, I was in denial. Since medical test results (data) do not lie, I realized my problem and changed my behaviour.

On my last birthday, I went to the hospital for a comprehensive checkup even though I did not have any medical complaints. An annual medical checkup was the best birthday gift I could give my body for a long and happy life. Since my birthday is already scheduled for every year, my medical exam is also scheduled. At my hospital, the medical staff mentioned that many people visit for preventive medical checkups annually. To me, there is no better way to celebrate my birthday.

In the past 3 years, I've spent more time on improving my health. I realize that I need to improve my quality of food, exercise regularly, and get sufficient sleep. Health deteriorates over a long time; it also improves only after a long time. To avoid unhealthy foods with friends, I joke with everyone that I'm planning on living for another 50 years. So, I have to avoid the *tasty* food. I'm healthier today than I was 10 years ago.

I visit my doctor immediately when I am sick. I found that many people avoid seeing a doctor unless they are really sick.

Here are some of my new habits. Most of them cost very little money:

- ❖ I drink 6–8 glasses of clean water (1.6 to 2 litres) a day. I am always sipping water. My trainer told me that if I wait to drink water when I am thirsty, it is too late. I am already dehydrated if I am thirsty.

✤ Install a 'reverse osmosis' water filter (much more effective than other water filters) at home to ensure clean water.

✤ I eat a fruit (guava, carrot, banana, tomato, papaya, apple) every 3 hours during the day. Tomatoes are my favorite fruit; they are one of the best and least expensive fruits around.[24] Great fruits need not cost a lot. Many people in India, including some doctors, believe that tomatoes increase risk for getting kidney stones. In my research, I found that tomatoes, because of their antioxidant properties, help prevent kidney stones.[25] I eat a variety of fruits since an excess of only one food item may be unhealthy.

✤ I avoid fried items such as samosa, dosa, etc. If I am stuck in a situation where only samosa or dosa is served, I ask the restaurant to reduce the oil used to prepare my meal if possible.

✤ I avoid all soft drinks, including Coca Cola and Pepsi, which are full of harmful sugar.

✤ I drink fresh coconut water as often as possible. Fresh coconut water is easily available in Mumbai and Hyderabad. To raise the awareness of our team members, we serve coconut water at the annual company team event instead of sugary soft drinks.

✤ I avoid alcoholic drinks. (I do not entertain others by making a fool of myself by getting drunk. Besides, I have a terrible hangover the next day.) We do not serve any alcohol at our company functions.

+ I wash hands with soap at least three times a day.

+ Nearly 20 years ago, my dentist told me that he wants me to die with my teeth intact. He mentioned that it is possible to avoid tooth loss if I take care of dental health. Every 6 months, I go to my dentist for dental cleaning and a dental checkup.

+ I have never smoked a cigarette or used tobacco. (Yes mother, it is true!) I am not sure what pleasures I may have missed. Many of my friends started smoking for various reasons (peer pressure, social rewards, and stress). Over the years, the news about the health damage caused by cigarette smoking keeps on getting worse. By not smoking, I also saved time and money.

+ I am glad that I avoid smoking completely. During my foreign trips, I do not bring cigarettes and liquor from airport customs duty-free shops as gifts for my relatives and friends. I reason that if I cannot offer vitamins, I should not facilitate a habit that is injurious to their health. I do not mind missing on the social reward. Now, I no longer get such requests.

+ While I am not a vegetarian, I avoid oily non-vegetarian curries, which used to taste really good to me. I am concerned about the health of the poultry and other animals used for non-vegetarian food. I find it easy to limit my cravings for non-vegetarian food.

❖ I eat breakfast every day. Earlier, I used to skip breakfast due to lack of time and various excuses. For the last 10 years, I've had oatmeal or low sugar cereal with milk for breakfast. I do not need to get my body into a starvation mode since I have not eaten since dinner. If nothing is easily available, I simply eat a banana or another fruit within 1 hour of waking up. I also eat two hard boiled eggs regularly for breakfast for protein and other nutrients.

❖ Some of my family members have a family history of certain diseases (diabetes, heart, asthma). Few act proactively to delay onset of these diseases.

Sugar is very unhealthy if not used in moderation. I have cut down on my sugar intake. Dr Robert Lustig, Professor of Medicine from the University of California at San Francisco, discusses sugar's negative effects in his famous YouTube video, *Sugar: The Bitter Truth*.[26] It is a popular video, which is also very educational.

Sugar is an acquired taste. Indians are genetically predisposed to Type-2 diabetes. According to medical experts, we have a diabetes epidemic coming due to our heavy consumption of sugar and fat (desi ghee) in sweets. Since learning about the coming diabetes epidemic, I help educate my co-workers, my friends, and my family members. At our company functions, we serve fresh fruits as an alternative to sweets.

When I was growing up, chocolate was unaffordable for the most part. I never developed a taste for chocolate. Good thing, I like to think. While pure chocolate is probably good for me, I do not miss the associated sugar.

Sleep is critical to staying healthy and not gaining weight. We need 8 hours of sleep each day. I turn off my cell phone before going to bed. I ask my family not to wake me unless there is an emergency. Whenever possible, I avoid early morning or late night travel on a regular basis. Exercise also helps me sleep better.

EXERCISE DAILY

The Human Performance Institute (HPI), a world-renowned research institute on fitness, developed a 7-minute exercise routine that requires no special equipment. The exercises do not require a membership to a gym. Comprised of 12 high intensity-effort exercises, the routine needs only body weight, a chair, and a wall. Each exercise is performed for 30 seconds, with 10 seconds of transition time. The entire circuit workout can be completed in 7 minutes. If we have energy left after 7 minutes, we can repeat the routine 2–3 times. The routine is equivalent to lifting weights and going for a long run.

Several people at our company started using these free techniques for daily exercise and report that they are exhausted in just 7 minutes. I used to say I had no time to exercise. Now I ask myself, 'Can I spend just 7 minutes every day to improve my health?' In many cases when I don't exercise, it's not because I lacked the time.

HPI has produced 20 Olympic Gold medalists across multiple sports, so their methodology and research is proven. A detailed article on the routine was published in the May-June 2013 issue of *The American College of Sports Medicine's Health & Fitness Journal*.[27] The article provides the routine for free and explains the science behind it. Anyone can follow these exercises by looking them up on the Internet.

Appendix-E lists the exercises with a picture and description for each.

Checklist for Healthy Habits

Daily

- Track your activity through mobile applications
- Track food calories through HealthifyMe
- Eat at home (cook your own meal if not living at home)
- Drink 6 glasses of water
- Sleep for 8 hours every day

Weekly

❖ Walk five times a week for 20 minutes per day (aerobic)

❖ Yoga or lift weights three times a week (resistance training)

Yearly

❖ Medical checkup, including a dietician visit

❖ Dental checkup

❖ Read at least one book on personal health

❖ Review health website newsletter subscription

Money

Most of us aspire to be rich one day. With a *disciplined* approach over *time*, it is easy to be rich. With tremendous professional opportunities available in the private sector, it is possible for us to do well financially.

In the first few years of my work, my income was very limited. I had many family obligations and educational loans. I had deferred many personal expenses. Once my paycheck became a regular monthly event, I felt increased peer pressure to enjoy life by buying a fancy car and shiny electronics. However, I remained disciplined and delayed gratification.

As I studied about money, I learned the difference between productive expenses (e.g., higher education) and unproductive expenses (e.g., restaurants, clothes, and vacations). I started saving early and regularly to take advantage of the tremendous power of compounding.

> 'Compound interest is the eighth wonder of the world. He who understands it, earns it...he who doesn't...pays it.'
>
> —ALBERT EINSTEIN

Besides compounding, I learned that taxes are our biggest single expense over our lifetime. Here are some ideas that helped me.

USE TAX FAVOURED SMALL SAVINGS SCHEMES

Personal taxes are our single biggest expense during our lives. As professionals, our income details are reported to the Income Tax Department, so we cannot avoid taxes. However, we owe it to ourselves to arrange our finances to *legally* minimize taxes. Our government offers tax incentives to encourage savings by individuals.

Simply, invest in tax-favoured schemes such as the Public Provident Fund (PPF) to defer taxes on long-term savings. All large employers offer an Employee Provident Fund (EPF) Scheme to help employees save money every month without paying any taxes now.

Many of our employees utilize the PPF scheme and deposit up to one lakh rupees every year at the State Bank of India or ICICI Bank. The PPF scheme currently pays 8.7 percent interest annually, which is tax free at withdrawal (typically 15 years or more). With tax-free compounding and guaranteed interest income, the account grows faster than many other investments. The PPF scheme is so attractive that our government limits individuals to investing only up to one lakh every year.

Even if you cannot deposit the entire limit of one lakh rupees every year, you can open an account with a minimum of one thousand rupees. To increase the interest income, many of our employees deposit the entire amount on April 1 of every financial year. It's very important to start saving early to take advantage of the power of compounding.

To increase savings among our employees, we offer our *Kaun Banega Crorepati* (Who wants to be a Millionaire; popularly known as KBC) challenge:

Which of the following two people will have more money at the age of 65? Veeru or Jai?

1. Engineer Jai deposits one lakh rupees every year from age 22 to age 29 for a total of eight lakhs in the PPF scheme. Jai does not deposit any additional money once he turns 30.
2. Engineer Veeru does not start saving until he is 30-years-old. Once Veeru turns 30, he deposits one lakh every year in the PPF scheme for the next 35 years for a total of thirty-five lakh rupees.

Most of our employees incorrectly select Veeru. At age 65, Jai will have ₹23,894,087 (29 times his deposits) and Veeru will have ₹23,817,130 (six times his deposits). Despite depositing more than four times as much as Jai, Veeru will have less money. Such is the power of tax-free compounding.

The table below summarizes the investment details. If you do not believe the results, Appendix-F provides the calculations behind the numbers.

TABLE 5.1: HOW 8 YEARS AT 22 CAN MAKE ALL
THE DIFFERENCE

	Jai	Veeru
Age when started saving	22	30
Years of Investment	8	35
Annual Interest Rate	8.7%	8.7%
Invested Amount (Principal)	₹800,000	₹3,500,000
Total Compound Interest	₹23,094,087	₹20,317,130
Total Maturity Amount	₹23,894,087	₹23,817,130

The irony is that when we are young and would benefit the most from saving, we do not have much money to save. Since our income is low, our taxes are low as well and we do not gain much from tax savings. We are also not thinking about retirement because it is 40 years away. As we get older, our income increases, but there is not as much time left until retirement. Without 40 years of compounding on our side, our money does not grow as much.

We encourage our employees to utilize the PPF scheme every year. To avoid hassles associated with EPF accounts, we steer our employees to use the PPF offered by State Bank and ICICI Bank. Presently, MAQ Software matches employee contributions to the PPF scheme. Employees can deposit up to one lakh rupees per year in their PPF accounts. The company provides up to fifty thousand rupees in matching contributions. With the income tax advantage, the PPF scheme is a great long-term saving option.

Over the past 25 years, I maximized my tax-free contributions to long-term savings plans. When I had to choose between personal expenses and long-term savings, I chose savings.

DEBT AND EXPENDITURES

By delaying expenses (and gratification), I avoid borrowing. I have borrowed money in my life, but for productive expenditures.

There are two kinds of expenditures: productive and consumption-oriented. A productive expenditure is good since it allows us to increase our income or assets (e.g., higher education, preventive medicine, books). A consumption-oriented expenditure does not help us build a financial base but does provide short-term pleasure (weekly movie tickets, latest Samsung S4 cell phone, and an expensive motorcycle when a cheaper option will work).

Many of us will eventually buy a house. Besides social status and comfort, a house provides financial discipline since we have to pay loan installments (EMI) every month to stay in the house. Before I purchased my house, I ensured that I had the necessary savings and income to afford interest payments. I realized that housing prices do not always go up faster than inflation. If I had over extended myself, other choices in my life may have been limited. In my view, a house is a lifestyle decision and is a consumption-oriented expenditure. If you take any investment where the growth is tax sheltered for 30 years, you will do well. However, many people lose because they fail to take into account the interest burden and the transaction cost of selling an illiquid investment (house). Tax deduction on the house's loan interest may not be enough to justify the added interest expense.

Many borrow for consumption expenditure using their credit card. I have never borrowed using a credit card even though it is easy to get a loan. Credit card loan interest rates are very high and I encourage everyone to avoid it. I simplify my life by carrying only *one* credit card and having only *one* bank account.

REDUCE TRANSPORTATION COSTS

I choose to live very close to work. My commute is always less than 10 minutes. Earlier in my life, I was lucky and lived in small towns where everything was close. After starting my career, I chose to compromise on the quality of my accommodation in favour of proximity to the office. Staying close to work saves me time and money, and is less stressful. I get extra time in the day every day. At our company, we had several very talented engineers who chose to live almost 1 hour away. In just a few years, they could not handle the stress and ended up leaving the company.

There are several benefits to reducing my commute. The first one is you reduce the time and stress that it takes to get to work. Second, by not driving, I reduce the probability of getting into accidents. That is why insurance companies ask me for the number of miles I drive annually to determine insurance rates. They reason that if I am not on the road, I cannot get into an accident. The third is that I minimize expenses. Driving is very expensive. Maintaining a car is very expensive. Moreover, it will only get worse with the price of petrol increasing.

The next question becomes finding a home close to work. For most people who live in large cities, it is *possible* to find a job and a place to live near each other. We can either compromise on the quality of housing or pay higher rent. I remember renting an apartment which was just minutes away from work. The good location required me to pay higher rent, and I had to adjust my other expenses. A similar apartment was available at a lower rent in a different locality further away from work. Later in my career, I remember buying a house which was very close to work. The house was old and was not as nice. For the same amount of money, I could have purchased a much nicer house far away, but I avoided family and peer pressure to do so.

So how has it benefitted me? If you look at the benefit my living close to work has created over 20 years, the compound effect has been huge. I have many friends who live very far from work. Over 20 years, several of them got into serious accidents that destroyed their cars and compromised their safety.

An alternative is to use public transportation as much as possible, which is safer and cheaper than using private transportation. However, public transportation in most major cities is slow, crowded, and inconvenient. When I was in Mumbai, I would take the train every day between 7.30 am and 7.45 am. A half hour later, the train would be full. If I left at 7.30 am, I avoided the crowd. I aligned my schedule to travel when few others were travelling.

Most people go to the office when it is the least efficient to travel. By getting to the office earlier, I avoided the crowds. It generally took a much shorter time. I was less stressed and I was much safer.

Then the second advantage was that by using quiet times on public transportation, I was able to catch up on my reading. Now, I listen to educational audio content. I use my time productively.

ON INVESTING IN THE STOCK MARKET

Since the reform in the early 1990s, the stock market in India has created enormous opportunities for companies to raise capital by selling shares. Before the 1990s, my parents could not easily invest in the stock market. Overall participation in the stock market by the general population and professionals was limited. With the convenience of the Internet and low cost trading, many individuals became active participants (day traders) in the stock market.

In the spring of 1993, during my final semester of MBA studies at the University of Michigan, I enrolled in a three credit class called 'Investments'. The class was taught by Professor Michael Wright, PhD, in the evening from 6 pm to 9 pm, once a week on every Wednesday. Professor Wright told all of the MBA students that the objective of the class was to teach students to 'buy low and sell high' in the context of the stock market. Professor Wright mentioned that buying low and selling high is extremely difficult in a stock market. Most active investors are unable to buy low and sell high even half (50 percent) of the time. He mentioned that if we could buy low and sell high even 50.1 percent of the time, we would be billionaires in no time. The reason that most active investors do not make money in the stock market is because they are competing with extremely informed stock trading professionals. As individual investors we lose.

During my MBA program, I also learned that risk and returns are highly related. As an investor, it is not possible to get higher returns, as compared to fixed deposits, without the risk of losing the principal investment (capital). In the late 1980s, many communities, including the Marwari and

Gujarati, offered loans to individuals at the rate of 3 percent interest per month (36 percent per annum). In comparison, bank deposits offered a 10–12 percent interest rate annually or even higher.

Even though my immediate family members did not have the capital to offer high interest loans, many in my extended family did offer high interest loans. Since these were informal transactions, there was also a tax advantage. Many of these lenders did not realize that this was a high risk loan.

One of my late uncles (Mamaji) became a money-lender as he saved some money (capital) through garment trading. Mamaji understood the perils of high risk and high risk interest loans. He mentioned to me that the borrower will agree to even an unreasonably high interest unsecured loan if he has no intention of returning the capital and interest. A lot of these so called 'loan sharks' really did not make much more than a bank fixed deposit once the risk associated with default was factored in.

In social conversations, once I started probing some of these extended family members who loaned money, they admitted that many of their high interest loans were never repaid. They lost their entire capital. Now, if I sat down with them and calculated their realized rate of return, it would be only marginally higher than the guaranteed bank interest.

So, the next question is how and where to invest money? If we have money left over after maximizing the tax advantaged PPF scheme, I consider stock and bond markets.

Historically, investing in the stock market has offered the highest risk adjusted return over a long period of time (greater than 20 years). The debt or debentures (bonds) issued by companies (public sector and private sector) and the government, offers lower risk and lower returns compared to the stock market.

Recently, I was discussing investments with one of our team members. He had joined MAQ Software's Mumbai office after completing his Computer Science degree from Mumbai University. He worked with us for 2 years. He left our company after 2 years to pursue an MBA program. After completing his MBA, he returned to MAQ Software to help lead projects.

During his engineering years, he joined a group of young engineers that were excited by the stock market. Typical of many engineers in our Mumbai office, he stayed at home with his parents. As a result, he was able to invest his take-home salary in the stock market. When I asked him about his experience with the stock market, he acknowledged that he had lost money there. He mentioned that among his stock trading friends, they keep trading until they lose all of their money. Just like gambling, it is hard for many to walk away with winnings when they are ahead. Buying and holding shares is not exciting. I suspect many engineers can avoid the stock market trap.

Professor Wright suggested that we must take a long-term (over 20-year view) of the stock market.

Next, he suggested that we should invest 95 percent of our investing money in a low-cost stock index fund. Low cost is important because many fund houses charge for buying and selling mutual funds to pay the selling investment advisor (broker). Professor Wright cautioned that the index fund approach is very boring since we only receive average returns. However, many active stock traders fail to get even the average returns offered by the overall stock market. For the fun and excitement aspect, he suggested using only 5 percent of our investable money in individual stocks for active trading. Use only 5 percent of the money as play money.

In the US, Vanguard offers a very low-cost S&P 500 stock index fund. In India, many low-cost index funds are available for purchase directly online. Over my career, I always invested in low-cost mutual funds and avoided trading stocks. Rising share markets make every investor look like a genius. The few stocks I did trade over the last 25 years, I wish I had avoided. I am unable to time the market. When I compare my timing of buying and selling stocks, I would have come out ahead with a broad stock market index fund with much lower risk.

As a result, during the last two severe economic downturns in 2000/2001 and 2008/2009, I was able to sleep peacefully. I was not an active participant in the market. I neither bought nor sold any shares or index funds. I bought a few shares of Citibank at what most thought was a 'bargain' price. Citibank shares have lost even more value and are a much better bargain. I lost money in trying to time the market. Overall, I let markets run their course. In the long run, I am ahead and stress free. I am able to focus on my profession instead of the stock market. I have realized that timing the stock market is very hard and most of us are not able to time so that we 'buy low and sell high'. Over the years, I have reflected on the lessons from the Investments class. Professor Wright was correct. I am glad that I had the discipline to follow his research.

In 1975, Charles D. Ellis wrote that investing is a 'Loser's Game' for most of us. Our results are determined more by errors than by successes. In the article, Ellis used a tennis analogy. He explained that professional tennis players win about 80 percent of their points through superior skill. Amateur tennis players lose about 80 percent of their points through errors. Amateur tennis is a loser's game because the person who makes the fewest mistakes wins.[28, 29]

Similarly, most people like me are only average badminton players. If I invite my co-worker to play badminton with me, both of us are likely to be average players. I can win the game just by making fewer mistakes. Most of us, average players, lose the badminton game because of our mistakes. The winner does not win because he hits great shots.

However, to win a US Open Tennis Tournament or a National Badminton Tournament, avoiding mistakes is not enough. The winner must also hit great shots.

Given that most of us are amateur investors (average players), we are our biggest enemy. We utilize investment opportunities to hurt ourselves badly. If we play long enough, we will eventually make mistakes. We should minimize the impact and the size of mistakes in our investing life. A similar approach is beneficial in life and company management.

Hearing about mistakes, most of us are paralyzed and are afraid to invest. We do not want to lose our hard-earned money. We are afraid of mistakes. So, we wait for stock markets to drop. Then, we buy shares of stocks that are in the news (retail, IT, real estate, and airlines in the recent past). We always hear, 'this time it is different'. All my life, I avoided the hot stock. I missed out on a few winners (say Google) at IPO. However, I avoided losing money by not investing in many companies that were considered sure winners.

The next question then is when should I purchase the low-cost stock index fund? Should I wait for the stock market to go down before investing? Or how can I time the stock market so that I buy the mutual fund at the lowest price?

My professors at the University of Michigan Business School researched these questions for the investors in the US. They showed that the stock market goes up for only a few days in a year. If we are not invested in the stock market on those days, our investment returns will be below the stock market average. For long-term investors, instead of waiting for markets to fall, they suggest investing immediately regardless of the market conditions.

I am not sure if the same research has been done for the stock market in India. I do not think that trying to time the stock market is possible for most of us.

I only invest in no-load low-cost index mutual funds. I do not check my returns on a daily basis. I know that in the long run, I will do well. In some areas of life, it is better to be boring.

ON LIFE INSURANCE

I avoided buying life insurance most my life. In India, the insurance sector was opened up in the last decade to allow the entry of private players. Many of these private sector insurance companies have teamed up with US insurance companies to offer attractive-sounding insurance schemes. Over the years, government-owned insurance companies (such as Life Insurance Corporation of India) offered insurance schemes which had income tax advantages.

Typically, I view life insurance as a way to cover expenses for my dependents (wife, children, and parents) if I die unexpectedly. Since I am not dependent on my young children for income, I have never purchased life insurance for my children. Insurance sales people are trained to use very emotional sales techniques to sell insurance for children. The line typically is 'Do you not love your children?' I do love my children. If they do die, I do not want the insurance company to pay me money.

The insurance industry offers a broad range of products to meet varying needs of people in different situations.

Very simply, I understand the following:

- Term life insurance requires me to pay monthly or annual installments. If I die within the insured period say, 65 years, my wife, and children will get a fixed amount (say fifty lakh rupees). If I do not die during the insured period, I do not get any money. Since life expectancy is greater than 50 years, this form of pure insurance is very inexpensive (generally, a few hundred rupees a month).

- Permanent life insurance is a combination of term life insurance and a savings scheme. Our payments to the insurance company cover a low interest bearing savings or investment portion, and a premium for the term life insurance portion. This is a hybrid product.

  In this plan, even if I do not die, I will get a fixed amount at the age of 65 from the low interest savings account. If I die before the policy maturity date, say my 50th birthday, my dependents get the full insured amount (say fifty lakh rupees) from the term life insurance portion. If you ask the insurance agent, they are selling the hybrid product in a single payment. The investment interest return is only about 3-4% (about half of the fixed deposit scheme).

Most products sold by insurance companies use a combination of these two approaches to cover individual situations.

When I did buy life insurance, I only purchased a very low-cost term life insurance plan offered as a group rate plan through my employers. I did not use a life insurance company to buy a low interest investment plan (permanent life or whole life). However, the risk with the employer plans is that if we lose our job later in our life (say 45 or 50 years old) and are sick, purchasing term life insurance may not be an option. Many insurance companies do not sell insurance to sick people at a reasonable price. I found it better to buy low-cost term life insurance individually. The plan I purchased did not depend on me assuming that the employer option would always be available.

I avoid buying expensive permanent life insurance (with low interest investment option) and use the money saved for higher interest paying investments. My wife can afford to live without my income since she also worked. Low-cost term life insurance generates very low profits and income for the insurance salesperson. Therefore they are reluctant to sell only the low-cost term life insurance.

Many of us are risk averse and want to avoid unpleasant situations. Therefore, if you must buy term life insurance for a few hundred rupees a month, consider using a low-cost online term life insurance provider, such as Religare or equivalent.

To increase their sales commission, which can amount to over 50 percent of the initial premiums, insurance agents use very effective sales techniques to sell poor investment schemes. These hybrid schemes offer poor rates of return and include low-cost term life insurance as part of a package. I can buy low-cost term life insurance by itself on my own. I do not need an insurance agent to sell me investments that offer half of the market rate of return.

ON HEALTH INSURANCE

We encourage all of our employees to carry adequate health insurance. Over the last 7 years, many new health insurance plans have been introduced by many public and private companies. Our company does not offer a group health insurance scheme in India. While there are advantages to group health insurance schemes for employees, our company elects to reimburse employees adequately for buying their own health insurance. By requiring employees to buy their own health insurance, we educate our employees about different types of insurance. Over the next 40 years of their career, I feel the information about their health insurance benefits will help them and their extended families.

I have seen many individuals suffer financially because they neglected to purchase health insurance.

Checklist for Money Habits

Daily

- Is this expense really necessary?
- Save money by eating food from home
- Is it a productive expenditure?
- Stay close to work

Monthly

- Review your paycheck for accuracy
- Review your bank statement
- Review your credit card statement
- Review monthly budget
- Deposit PPF installment

Yearly

- Use one bank account and one credit card
- Review your tax return to find areas to save taxes
- Keep copies of Form 16 and income tax return

6

Final Thoughts

'The difference between successful people and very successful people is that very successful people say "no" to almost everything.'

—WARREN BUFFET
Investor and philanthropist

As I gained experience and confidence, I learned to say 'no' most of the time. When I say 'no' to an invitation, I am saying 'yes' to something else. Recently, I had an option to watch a professional soccer game live, which would have taken up 4 hours, including the travel. Instead, I chose to relax at home and go out for a family dinner.

On Sunday, I chose to go for a walk with a friend for nearly an hour. During the walk, I was able to catch up with him socially and also discuss industry matters. In addition to physical exercise, I developed myself professionally. My alternative was to stay at home and watch TV. As I have started these activities, I find other like-minded people who like to stay fit and grow professionally.

In my discussions with young engineers, many tell me that I am describing a very boring life. What about having fun and enjoying life today?

Focussing on key activities in a *disciplined* manner over the years has enabled me to enjoy life. Until I became disciplined and focussed, I did not advance to the next stage of my life. Every time I had to change, it was very hard for me, initially. However, once I practiced, my mental and physical resistance disappeared.

People stress the importance of following your true passion and purpose in life. If I am like most people, I do not have a clue what my 'true purpose' is. Worse, I do not even know how to find my passion or purpose in life. In my view, successful people choose to love the job they are working in. While we are waiting to find our passion and purpose in life, we need to be passionate about whatever job we have today.

People consider me very lucky. In *Great by Choice*, Jim Collins mentions that *return on luck*[30] is more important than luck. He asserts that a lucky event has to meet three criteria. It has to be independent of my actions, have significant consequences (good or bad), and be unpredictable. I do not know that I was luckier than most, but I certainly had a high return on luck. While I did not depend on good luck, I did take advantage of opportunities to grow when they became available.

As we discussed earlier in the book, nothing ever changes in my life unless I take action. I hope that by sharing my examples, you will select alternatives *deliberately*.

7

Seven Decisions

'The hardest decisions in life are not between good and bad or right and wrong, but between two goods or two rights.'

—JOE ANDREW
American politician and lawyer

Over my life, I've had to make choices. All of my decisions fell into these seven areas.

1. What do I study or what profession do I choose?
2. Where do I choose to live?
3. Whom do I marry?
4. How do I spend my income?
5. How many children do I have?
6. How do I take care of my health and spirituality?
7. What do I do to help others?

There is no *right* or *wrong* answer for any of these questions. My life would be different if I had selected a different answer. Not better or worse, just *different*. Many of these decisions are irreversible.

Most of us are called to make these decisions when we are between 18 and 30 years of age. All of these choices impact our use of scarce and precious resources of time and money, and have a huge compound effect.

In my discussions, people ask me, 'Is there any one decision that is more significant than the other six?' An American author, H. Jackson Brown Jr., stated, 'Choose your life's mate carefully. From this one decision will come 90 percent of all your happiness or misery.'

In my experience also, the choice of life partner (husband or wife) is more significant than the rest of the decisions. Most people spend 30–50 years in the company of the same person. My thinking, habits, and decisions were influenced and shaped by my spouse. If my spouse did not learn and grow over time, I would not be able to advance as time progresses.

8

Admirations

'I would maintain that thanks are the highest form
of thought; and that gratitude is happiness doubled
by wonder.'

—GILBERT K. CHESTERTON
English writer and art critic

'Dedicated to the Service of the Nation' is displayed prominently over the grandiose entrance of IIT Kharagpur. I admire Jawaharlal Nehru for converting a British Raj remnant Hijli jail in rural West Bengal to the very first IIT. I wonder about the choices and sacrifices made by a newly independent nation to fund such an institute right after independence. Over my 5 years at Kharagpur, I entered my adulthood in the company of some of the brightest people I have ever met in my life. I still admire many of you. All of you taught me a lot, so thank you. Sometimes, I wonder how your journey turned out.

I still wonder how my teachers put up with me while I was preparing for the seemingly impossible

IIT JEE. I admire Shiv Shankar Tripathi, my 11th and 12th grade GIC teacher, for tutoring me in Mathematics and Physics. Without your patience in working with esoteric JEE problems, I would be running a flourishing criminal law practice in Shahjahanpur today. Despite the justified skepticism of your fellow teachers about my JEE aspirations, you never doubted me. I thank you.

I also thank Budh Bara Singh, my 9th and 10th grade teacher, for tutoring me in Mathematics and Physics. I appreciate you accepting me as a student even though you were not supposed to accept any new students that year. It meant a lot to me. I can still visualize your rented room where your wooden cot (charpai) and a wooden bench served well for our tuitions. I remember riding my bicycle during cold winters on dark unlit roads to your 5 am tuition class, before the winter sun rose. My bike ride felt longer due to the cold and wet morning dew. And because my hands used to be numb and nearly frozen, I am not sure if the fear of your two-foot long wooden cane (danda) striking my palm had any effect on me completing my homework. From what I remember, you spared me the danda on most days. Magically, homework was completed every day. That danda had magic. Dozens of today's doctors and engineers experienced the magic of the danda during their high school years. I wonder if the danda still has its magic. I know you meant well.

To the Sahai family in Webster City, Iowa, who adopted me and made my 5 years in Iowa the best part of my life. Prem Nath Sahai, PhD was like a father to me. Uncleji, you taught me that learning never goes to waste. I wish the Heavens would have waited longer for you. I miss you. Urmilla Sahai, my other mother and Auntieji who has seen the most joys and most hardships I have ever witnessed anyone handle in one life. I am amazed at your calmness. To the Sahai kids, who are now all surgeons and physicians and have spouses. I am amazed at all of you for blending the best of east and west.

To Subhash Jijaji and Sushma didi, who adopted me as their little brother. I admire both of you for sharing so much energy and affection with everyone. I wish to be like you when I grow up. To my late Anil Jijaji who did so much in such a short life—from getting a doctorate in Electrical Engineering to becoming a compassionate physician; for completing one of the most beautiful temples anywhere; for inventing and selling pill dispenser MD2 machines to Philips—today's startups can learn a lot from you. To my Nutan didi, the always cheerful Social Director.

To Varsha and Dilip Naik for being true friends, and for the support you have provided to me and everyone in the community.

Sanjiv Rastogi for being the older brother I never had. You and Rajani amaze me for always thinking of carrying everyone forward.

To my Sushma Mausiji and Sarvesh Mausaji, I admire you for your love and affection every day. To my Sajjan Mamaji and Manju Mamiji for being the role model early in my life. I admire you for your affection for all of us.

My parents, Rajendra Saran Agarwal and Daya Agarwal, still amaze me by being able to raise four of us in Shahjahanpur. Your determination in supporting the four of us in Tier-1 professional colleges astounds me. You have set such a high bar that I am not sure if I will be able to match you.

To my brother Sanjeev Agarwal, MD and his wife, Chhavi Agarwal, MD who paid their dues and became some of the best in their chosen medical fields. Your calmness amazes me.

To my not-so-little brother, now a serial entrepreneur, Pankaj Agarwal and his wife Rita Agarwal for teaching me what the corporate world did not teach me about business. I am amazed at how you can start so many companies and not lose money. Thank you for being a good friend and keeping such high spirits all the time. I learn a lot from you.

To my sister Mudita and my brother-in-law Mohit Gupta, for understanding me and keeping everyone together.

To my in-laws, Vishnu Prakash Agarwal and Vinod Rani Agarwal, for being there for us. You taught me that parenting never ends. To Vijay Kumar Agarwal and Ajay Kumar Agarwal for being great souls in mobilizing the resources to complete the Science section at Arya Mahila Intermediate College, Shahjhanpur. Over 2,000 girls have had the opportunity to learn mathematics and science due to your help. To Namita and Rajesh Jiwrajka for your affection and caring. To Aparna and Manesh Gupta for the support and milestone visits. To Ashish and Prerna for your care and affection.

To my dozen nephews and nieces: Disha, Rishi, Abhay, Nikhil, Amit, Anushka, Malika, Ashna, Eshana, Neil, Anika, and Myra. You set a high bar every day. I am proud of every one of you.

To Arpita, my wife and partner in the game of work and business of life. I am still amazed at how you took a chance on me. I admire your leadership and how you make it all work.

To my children, Jay Raj and Shelly Ranie, for being the critics I need to stay grounded. I hope that you will agree with Mark Twain in a few years. He said, 'When I was a boy of 14, my father was so ignorant I could hardly stand to have the old man around. But when I got to be 21, I was astonished at how much the old man had learned in 7 years.' I am working on learning. You have miles to go.

To all of my friends and colleagues who have supported me over the years. Thank you!

'Inspiration is for amateurs.
The rest of us just show up and get to work.'

—CHUCK CLOSE
American painter

APPENDIX-A

Master Checklist

Campus to Workplace Transition

- Learn about the department and the company
- Speak to alumni in the company and the city
- Review core subjects in Computer Science, including Data Structures and Databases

Managing Work

- Limit use of text messaging, cell phone, Facebook, Twitter, e-mail to few times a day
- Avoid distractions at work
- Schedule 6 months to 1 year in advance
- Be on time to the office
- Track items to closure
- Follow team standards
- Start meetings on time
- End meetings on time
- Go to your boss with solutions, not just problems

- Help your boss with their challenges
- Inform IT department of needs ahead of time
- Read employee manual

Personal Effectiveness

- Read two industry-related books per month
- Read industry magazines
- Watch industry lectures
- Plan leaves 6 months in advance
- Attend company events
- Avoid busy traffic times
- Practice English daily for 10 minutes—both verbal and written
- Use correct eating utensils
- Dress conservatively
- Dress for the weather
- Always wear shoes
- Own a set of formal clothes
- Keep a 'thank you' mindset

Healthy Habits

Daily

- Track your activity through mobile applications
- Track food calories
- Eat at home (cook your own meal if not living at home)

- Drink 8 glasses of water
- Sleep for 8 hours every day

Weekly

- Walk five times a week for 20 minutes per day (aerobic)
- Yoga or lift weights three times a week (resistance training)

Yearly

- Medical checkup, including a dietician visit
- Dental checkup
- Read at least one book on personal health
- Review health website newsletter subscription

Money

Daily

- Is this expense really necessary?
- Save money by eating food from home
- Is it a productive expenditure?
- Stay close to work

Monthly

- Review your paycheck for accuracy
- Review your bank statement
- Review your credit card statement
- Review your monthly budget

+ Deposit PPF installment

Yearly

+ Simplify life, only *one* bank account and *one* credit card

+ Review income tax return to find areas to save taxes

+ Keep copies of Form 16 and income tax return

APPENDIX-B

Suggested Reading

Over 50,000 new business books were published in the last 10 years. Many of these books are easy to read and can be completed in a few hours.

When I meet with key leaders, often the first question we ask each other is, 'What book are you reading these days?' In fact, this is also one of my first interview questions as an employer. By reviewing the list of books they like or remember, I learn a lot about a candidate.

In my review of books, I selected 10 authors who helped me grow over the years. A lot of their work is based on empirical research and studies of companies. As a practicing manager, I like their 'how to' approach and how we can apply the lessons in them at our company.

If there is only *one* book I ask new hires to review before they join our company, it is *The First 90 Days* by Michael Watkins. A revised edition was recently released by Harvard Business School Press.

Management

1. *Good to Great* and/or *Built to Last*[31] by Jim Collins

If there was only one author today who has had the most impact on management, it would be Jim Collins. His first book, *Built to Last: Successful Habits of Visionary Companies,* is relevant for many companies that are in early stages. In this great book, Collins explains how long-term sustained performance can be engineered. I read *Good to Great* in 2003 when the book came out. At that time, our company was younger and smaller, and we were struggling to stay in business. In 2003, the concepts and ideas mentioned in *Good to Great* were ahead of our company stage. In 2007, when our company had expanded, I read *Good to Great* again. Many of the ideas in his book are now our operating principles. By implementing these ideas in a disciplined and consistent manner, we have grown the company over time.

His latest book, *Great by Choice,* is also relevant and shares many counterintuitive examples from very successful companies. We require all new MBA graduates joining our company to review *Good to Great* tools.

2. *The Speed of Trust,*[32] by Stephen M. R. Covey

We have been using this book for the last 5 years within our leadership team to improve trust within the organization. Stephen M. R. Covey offers 12 techniques that helped me improve my effectiveness in the team. I found this book to be an easier read compared to *The Seven Habits of Highly Effective People* written by his late father, Stephen R. Covey.

3. *Who: The A Method for Hiring,*[33] by Geoff Smart and Randy Street

In this book, the authors present the 'A' method for hiring. The authors interviewed 300 CEOs and 20 billionaires to understand successful hiring techniques. In my experience, many successful corporate recruiters are familiar with these recruitment techniques. Another, larger book is *Topgrading*, written by Geoff Smart's father, Bradford D. Smart, who used to advise legendary and longtime GE CEO, Jack Welch. The Indian edition of *Topgrading* is available in many bookstores.

4. *First, Break All the Rules: What the World's Greatest Managers Do Differently,*[34] by Marcus Buckingham

For this book, the author surveyed 80,000 managers to understand what great managers have in common. At MAQ Software, we practice techniques used in the book to turn employee talent into performance. From the book, we use 12 simple questions to seek opinions at our regular employee meetings. I found lessons in this book useful for our team leads and senior managers. There are critical performance and career lessons that I was able to apply in the context of our company.

5. *People Styles at Work,*[35] by Robert and Dorothy Bolton

Published by The American Management Association for Practicing Managers, this book covers four different types of people styles. Even though I have gone through many personality tests, including MBTI and DISC, this book helped me understand my behaviours and how I could adjust them to people of different styles.

By using knowledge gained in our professional and personal relationships, we have increased our effectiveness and are able to resolve conflicts more easily.

6. *The First 90 Days,*[36] by Michael Watkins

We share this book with all of our new MBA graduates and people hired from the industry. Author Michael Watkins is an expert on leadership transitions. Although this book is written for very senior level executives in large companies, it helps our new hires realize that they need to take time to understand the context of our work, our clients, and our people and make necessary adjustments.

As the book explains, there is little value added by the new hire in the first 6 months. The typical contribution of a new hire is negative in the first 90 days, and enters positive area only in the second 90 days, resulting in net zero contribution in the first 6 months. The author also explains the increasingly demanding professional landscape, where managers face frequent transitions and very high expectations.

Checklists and self-assessments are included in each chapter to help readers apply key lessons to their own situations.

7. *How To Be an Even Better Manager*,[37] by Michael Armstrong

Unlike most books on management and leadership, this concise and actionable book includes many useful 'how to' techniques for supervisors in our company. I have benefited tremendously from the comprehensive positive and negative indicators table for behaviour common in all industries.

Many employees ask for feedback on a regular basis. I usually share the positive and negative indicators with them to help them do a self-assessment. I also use the indicators to improve my own performance. I have seen people recognize their own behaviours that were limiting their performance and growth in the company.

8. *Emotional Intelligence 2.0*,[38] by Travis Bradberry

We hire people who are very intelligent (high IQ with engineering and MBA-degree combination) and have a relevant role-related personality (work style). Current thinking states that most people are born with a certain level of IQ that does not change over their life. Similarly, personality traits appear early in life and they do not go away.

The book includes 66 techniques to improve our emotional intelligence (EQ). I review this book every quarter to help me improve my EQ. It is an easy and short read with an online test to help measure EQ.

Personal

9. *YOU: The Owner's Manual,*[39] by Dr Oz

Before first reading this book 5 years ago, I knew more about my cell phone than I knew about my body. This book helped me learn about my own body, the food I eat, common illnesses and ways to avoid them.

As I aged, I saw that my friends suffer from heart disease, diabetes, and cancer. Asthma is quite common, but usually does not kill us. As I started thinking about the next 50 years of my life, I realized I did not have a plan for staying fit and healthy. As I came across successful people in any field, I realized that they were also fit and had the stamina to perform at a high level. This helped me become disciplined and improve my quality of life. I now live a much healthier lifestyle.

10. *The Success Principles,*[40] by Jack Canfield

This book lists over 64 principles that helped me learn great leaders' practices and behaviours. Jack Canfield has had seven books on the bestseller list simultaneously, which is extremely difficult to do.

A smaller book, *The Power of Focus*, mentioned to me by my serial entrepreneur brother, is another one of my favourite books by the same author. One of the ideas mentioned in the book is to surround yourself with successful and positive people (avoid toxic people). As a result of reading the book, I actively seek out positive friends.

APPENDIX-C

E-mail and IM

'Put it before them briefly so they will read it, clearly so they will appreciate it, picturesquely so they will remember it, and, above all, accurately so they will be guided by its light.'

—JOSEPH PULITZER
American journalist

E-mail and Instant Messaging (IM) are forms of formal business communication. Companies, including ours, use them to communicate with co-workers and clients. I encourage our engineers to write every project-related e-mail as if it is customer ready and can be forwarded to the client. Nowadays, e-mail and, more often, IM are used for professional communication similar to an in-person business meeting or a formal business phone call.

When I graduated from college, e-mail was not commonly available or widely used in the industry. In the early 1990s, if I sent an e-mail to someone, I used to phone that person right afterward and verify if they had checked their e-mail. Next, I would ask them if they had received my e-mail since e-mail was not always delivered. Over the last 20 years, e-mail has become a reliable and affordable form of communication.

Our company, like many others, uses e-mail heavily to run our operations. For the discussion below, I use modern e-mail systems and Microsoft Outlook interchangeably. Most modern e-mail systems offer comparable functions.

With time, our industry has developed our own set of expectations and behaviours concerning e-mail. In sending and receiving over five lakh messages over the last 20 years, I have made almost all of the common mistakes below. However, different companies have different cultures around e-mail use. For new people joining the industry who never used any typewriters, they find it odd that Outlook uses abbreviations that refer to the pre-software era.

Some of my mistakes and experiences are discussed below:

1. In the 'To:' section, I try to address my e-mail message to only one person. Otherwise, it is unclear who is supposed to work on the e-mail. I used to put many recipients in the 'To:' section and as a result, nothing got done. As the old saying goes, '*Everybody* was sure that *Somebody* would do it. *Anybody* could have done it, but *Nobody* did it.' When I followed up, everybody thought that somebody was working on it. Now, I expect that the person

in the 'To:' line is accountable for acting and responding to my message.

2. The 'CC:' line provides me with an opportunity to add additional recipients. I add additional people on the 'CC:' line (which stands for 'carbon copy' and is left over from the typewriter days) to avoid the 'no one told me' response. I ensure that as many recipients as possible are added in the 'CC:' line so that they can intervene if they notice a problem or blocking issue with my request.

3. The 'BCC:' line stands for 'Blind Carbon Copy.' Blind copying implies that I do not want the people in the 'To:' line and 'CC:' line to know that I am sending this e-mail to someone else. Those who I blind copy may wonder why I do not want the other recipients to know that I sent them a copy. Worse, the person who received my BCC may 'Reply All' to my e-mail offering their response to a controversial or confidential issue. I have learned to never use the 'BCC:' line. I discourage everyone in our company from using the 'BCC:' line.

   If I want to inform someone about a topic, I include them in the 'CC:' line. Or, I forward them the message separately.

4. The 'subject' line provides the opportunity for the sender to specify the message's intent. I encourage every message to be action oriented. I ask our engineers to start e-mail subject lines with a verb. Common verbs include review,

approve, inform, reject, send, provide, and confirm. Placing these simple verbs at the beginning of the subject line forces the sender to think clearly about the desired outcome of their e-mail message.

For example, if I want someone to provide a report by 5 pm, my subject line reads 'Need deployment report by 5 pm'. My subject line does not read 'Report'.

Most current e-mail systems (e.g., Outlook 2013) display a warning message when the sender is sending a message with a blank subject line. Leaving the subject line blank in e-mail messages is a common mistake by new users.

5. I fill in the To:, CC:, and subject lines after composing e-mail, not first. With blank To:, CC: and subject lines, if I accidently hit 'send' before my e-mail message is typed or edited, Outlook gives an error message. The error message helps me avoid sending incomplete messages where I look bad.

6. The 'message preview' feature in e-mail systems displays the first three lines (about 40 to 50 words) without requiring the recipient to open the message. Many executives receive large numbers of messages. I learned to summarize my e-mail in the first three lines so that the reader does not have to work hard and read the entire message.

7. I write e-mail messages from the recipient's point of view. If I am sending a meeting request, I convert the time to the recipient's time zone so that the recipient does not have to do math. For example, if I am suggesting a meeting time, I include the recipient's local time first. Next, I also add my time zone e.g., 11 am EST (8 am PST). Often, I receive meeting requests for 11 am from senders in New York (3 hours ahead). Now, I am confused and must send a follow up message to clarify the actual meeting time. Meeting requests in Outlook automatically convert to the correct time zone as long as the computer is set up correctly.

   Many times, we respond to US clients for expected completion of a task in India time. For example, we may tell a US client our task will be completed at 5 pm IST. Our clients then have to convert the time to their local time. Let's do the extra work and think from the client's point of view.

8. 'If you do not want it to go anywhere, do not put it in e-mail' was a favourite saying of my Group Administrator when I was at Microsoft. I was new to e-mail and a new employee. She was right. My messages get forwarded to people I would never imagine. Without proper context, some of these messages can be misconstrued by readers.

9. In any fast-paced industry, almost every group situation invariably generates conflict. One of

my first bosses always advised me to de-escalate instead of sending a sarcastic or angry e-mail. While I did not always follow his advice, I learned to control my emotions. I do not respond when I am angry. Once I hit the send button, it is hard to take back those words.

One of our project managers uses two techniques. First, if his e-mail message sounds too irate, he will save a draft and ignore it for 8–24 hours. When he comes back to the e-mail message, he ends up rewording it almost 100 percent of the time. Second, he has a rule in his Outlook that delays all sent mail by one minute. That allows him to change his mind and reword something or add additional information after he hits send. The release manager who recommended this to him has her delay rule set to 2 minutes.

10. I reply to e-mail messages the same day. Everyone expects it. In fact, in my e-mail interactions with very senior people (CEOs and VPs of large companies), they respond promptly to everyone. Even if their answer is 'no,' responsiveness has helped them get ahead. People feel heard and acknowledged.

I sometimes receive e-mail messages for which I need to do additional research or contact additional people. It may take me days before I can fully address the request. In such situations, I respond to the sender and let them know that I have read their e-mail. Next,

I let them know that I am working on their request and when they can expect my complete response.

11. I do not start a new e-mail message when I am responding to an earlier request. If someone is responding to my earlier request, I appreciate if they respond to the previous message on the subject. As a reader, I am able to scroll down and can understand the context. I avoid my laziness and search for the prior e-mail on the topic and provide the information. Inexperienced users commonly neglect to do this.

12. I do not discuss multiple unrelated topics in one e-mail message. In my work, I may interact with a person on multiple subjects which are unrelated. Many people put all of the unrelated subjects in a single e-mail message which creates problems for the receiver. Usually, the receiver forwards the message to another person or a group to gather input. If there are unrelated messages in a single e-mail, it may be inappropriate to forward the entire e-mail to the next group.

For example, I had two unrelated topics to discuss with one of our project managers. First, I was discussing an application that was running slow for one of our clients. She had complained to me about the application speed. I needed to follow up with that project manager. Second, I also needed to coordinate my leave plans with the project manager and coordinate leave plans for key managers. I sent two distinct e-mail messages. In my first e-mail to the project manager, I only discussed the slow application performance. The project manager could forward that e-mail with his comments to the engineering team. In the second e-mail message, I sought his input regarding my leave plans.

An e-mail message is different from an in person meeting. If I am meeting the project manager, I will sequentially discuss both these topics in one meeting. After the meeting, the project manager will follow up on the application speed with the engineering team. For the leave plans, the project manager may provide his input during the meeting itself.

13. I avoid slang in my e-mail messages. Common words and phrases to avoid include ya'll, yeah, bummed out, gonna, damn, bummer, freak out, jerk, what's up, wimp, dude, buddy, hey, and dough. Earlier in my life, when I had limited or poor vocabulary, I did not understand that these words were slang and made some poor impressions as a result.

14. For really important e-mail messages (reaching over 50 people), I print and read my message before I send it. Next, I ask a co-worker to read my message for any errors.

15. As with all good writing, I keep e-mail messages short and to the point.

16. When answering an e-mail message, I use proper context. For a business manager, I

do not give too many technical details. For a technical reader, I provide all of the necessary technical information.

17. I do not use the exclamation point (!) or exclamation points (!!!) in my e-mail messages. They denote extraordinary excitement or surprise. This is a common mistake.

18. The 'Reply All' button ensures that everyone included in my original e-mail message receives my response. I prefer to use 'Reply All' instead of a simple 'Reply'. If the original sender decided to include others, there must be a reason for the sender to include them. I don't want to create suspense for some people.

19 When anyone joins our company, they are added to certain e-mail distribution lists (or aliases or groups). Some of these distribution lists include hundreds of people. When I do 'Reply All' to a message, I pay attention to which distribution lists are large. To prevent spam and abuse of e-mail lists, our IT team limits who can send messages to large distribution lists.

Years ago, I was part of an e-mail distribution list that had over 10,000 people. One user sent an e-mail that was not appropriate for such a large group. Another person saw that message and asked the original sender to not use such a large distribution list. Unfortunately, he did use 'Reply All'. Within minutes, additional people were responding to the message by asking everyone else to not use 'Reply All'. Within a few hours, there were hundreds of messages sent to thousands of people, which clogged the e-mail servers. Everyone was annoyed and this situation created new awareness about the dangers of the 'Reply All' button.

20. I err on the side of over communicating and not under communicating. I over communicate by ensuring that more people are included in the e-mail message than absolutely necessary (while still minding distribution lists).

21. I set up my Outlook signature in my computer. My signature always provides my complete contact information, including my cell phone number, in all of my e-mail messages. In the last 14 years, I have received less than 10 unsolicited sales calls on my cell phone as a result of sharing my contact information. On the positive side, our clients always had access to me in case they needed to reach me. I feel better that they can reach me. I am surprised that many people in sales and customer service roles do not include their full contact information in their e-mail messages. I have to work extra hard in the rare instances when I have to reach them.

22. Many people in our company are taught to colour code messages from important people or topics. I have yet to use colour coding, probably because I have been working with the same group of people for many years. I recognize e-mail message patterns of key

people in the company. For new hires, colour coding messages may be useful.

23. I do not use 'inspirational' or otherwise quotes in my e-mail signature. Many perceive them as condescending.

24. I DO NOT USE CAPITAL LETTERS IN E-MAIL MESSAGES. It is equivalent to shouting and I perceive the sender as angry. In the typewriter days, people used CAPITAL LETTERS to emphasize an issue. Now, we can use font formatting (size, colour, underline, bold, etc.) for emphasis. Every so often, I receive an e-mail message from a junior employee in CAPITAL LETTERS.

25. Always check e-mail messages before sending for spelling and grammar mistakes. I lose credibility if my message contains spelling and grammar mistakes. If an engineer sends me an e-mail with spelling mistakes, I automatically assume that they lack attention to detail and their work is sloppy. To avoid spelling mistakes, I turn on the 'Check Spelling' option before sending in Outlook. Once turned on, Outlook checks spelling every time I hit the send button for a message.

26. I recheck the e-mail addresses before I send the e-mail. Outlook and other systems try to help the sender by auto filling part of the e-mail address. I have sent confidential information by mistake because I was not paying attention.

It took me a long time to recover from this mistake.

27. My work e-mail is my work e-mail. I use it only for work-related purposes. Most of us now have free e-mail accounts on Outlook.com, Gmail, and others. I educate my social friends to send unrelated information to my non-work e-mail account.

28. Outlook allows end-users to send normal, low, and high priority e-mail. I rarely use 'High' priority e-mail, which signifies emergencies to me. For example, if a critical computer system has broken down and is causing production problems, I expect to receive a 'High Priority' e-mail with a red flag in Outlook. I routinely see certain individuals send only 'High Priority' e-mail which conveys their immaturity and attention-seeking nature to me. I do not send more than one 'High Priority' red flag e-mail in a month. Over time, we have trained our engineers to use the 'High Priority' button sparingly. I use 'Low Priority' e-mail messages more often. For example, if I have to inform the team that snacks are in the kitchen, I use the 'Low Priority' flag since that information is not critical. Not everyone cares about the snacks.

29. Outlook includes e-mail 'Read Receipt' feature to notify the sender that the receiver has read the message. I get a lot of sales related

SPAM e-mail. I do not send 'Read Receipt' acknowledgment to anyone. If I receive an unsolicited sales e-mail from outside the company, I do not want to let spammer know that I read their e-mail. For e-mail sent by someone within the company using the company e-mail service, I am expected to read every e-mail message. There is no need for me to send any 'Read Receipt'. If I have something urgent where I need positive confirmation, I visit that person or phone that person.

30. I do not use colour wall paper as the e-mail background. Outlook by default comes with a white background. I use the simple and clean white color background, which allows me and the reader to focus on the message.

31. Emoticons ☺ to convey emotions have become more common and accepted in the industry. However, I do not use emoticons.

32. I do not open an e-mail attachment unless it comes from a trusted person. Opening an e-mail containing a virus can do serious harm to your computer.

33. For controversial issues, resolving problems in person is better. Instead of sending e-mail, meet with the person and talk. If you cannot meet with them, phone the other person.

34. Outlook includes a Message Recall feature that allows us to recall our messages. In my experience, this feature does not work across all systems.

35 I use 'Contacts' in Outlook to record the phone numbers, postal addresses, and e-mail addresses of key relatives and friends. Over the years, my mobile phones have changed. Many addresses are still the same and transferred over to the new phones without any effort. While travelling, I keep a printed copy of Outlook contacts with me in case I need to reach someone and my mobile phone's battery is dead.

Many of the above rules apply to Instant Messages and text messages (SMS), which are used for quick and informal communication. With co-workers and clients, I tend to use formal English.

Checklist for E-mail Messages

- Fill in To:, CC:, and Subject line after writing the e-mail message.
- Check To: and CC: to include key people
- Use a verb as the first word in Subject line
- Check spelling and grammar before sending an e-mail message
- Set up signature in Outlook
- Use existing e-mail discussion on an existing topic
- Review message carefully for clarity and conciseness

APPENDIX-D

Commonly Misused Words

The following words are commonly confused with each other. Many of these words have very similar-looking spelling so our minds gloss over them. Since Microsoft Office applications do not highlight them as a misspelled word, these mistakes are more difficult to catch. With practice and reading, I have trained myself to catch them quickly.

ACCEPT, EXCEPT

+ I **accept** your invitation. (receive, approve, tolerate)
+ **Except** for emergencies, employees should always arrive on time. (excuse)

ADAPT, ADOPT

+ I have to **adapt** to market conditions. (adjust to)
+ I have to **adopt** the culture and learn the language. (choose as one's own)

AFFECT, EFFECT

+ Poems **affect** me deeply. (move, influence)

+ Writing papers has a strange **effect** on me. (result)

+ The government wants to **effect** a low inflation policy. (bring about)

ASSURE, ENSURE, INSURE

+ He **assured** us that everything would turn out alright. (promise)

+ I want to **ensure** my projects succeed. (guarantee, make sure)

+ We do our best to **insure** ourselves against fire. (secure against harm)

BESIDE, BESIDES

+ He stood **beside** the car. (by)

+ **Besides** samosa, he did not like any north-Indian dishes. (except)

+ I enjoyed the salad. **Besides,** it was healthy for me. (moreover)

COACH, COUCH

+ Can you **coach** me to play cricket like Sachin? (teach)

+ I sat on the **couch** to watch TV. (sofa)

CITE, SIGHT, SITE

✦ A good research paper will **cite** more than one authority on a subject. (use as proof)

✦ Amitabh Bachchan was in the moviegoers' line of **sight**. (vision, act of seeing)

✦ Raj Ghat is the **site** of a memorial to Gandhi. (location)

COMPLEMENT, COMPLIMENT

✦ Riti's shoes **complement** her dress. (completion)

✦ I **complimented** Riti on her shoes. (praise)

DISCREET, DISCRETE

✦ He was **discreet** about his co-worker's performance review. (carefully quiet)

✦ She provided two **discrete** examples. (separate, distinct)

FEWER, LESS

✦ **Fewer** people than last year voted. (fewer in number)

✦ **Less** money was donated than they expected. (less in amount)

IMPLY, INFER

✦ The speaker **implies** the economy is growing. (suggests)

✦ The hearer **infers** that the speaker believes the economy is growing. (gathers, concludes)

ITS, IT'S

+ The dog scratched **its** ears. (possessive)
+ **It's** a sunny day. (Combination of it and is)

LEAD, LED, LEAD

+ He was asked to **lead** the project. (be in charge)
+ Once upon a time he **led** the group to the river. (guided)
+ After walking six miles up a mountain, his feet felt like **lead**. (a heavy metal)

LOSE, LOOSE

+ I don't want to **lose** the gold chain. (loss)
+ My shoe is **loose**. (too big for my feet)

PRINCIPLE, PRINCIPAL

+ I support your **principle**, but I disagree with your methods. (aim, ideal)
+ My high-school **principal** was very intelligent. (head of a school)
+ Smoking was the **principal** cause of his lung cancer. (main, chief)
+ The **principal** earned ₹200 interest. (capital sum)

THEN, THAN

+ First I will wash my hands, **then** I will eat.
+ I like tomatoes more **than** potatoes. (comparative)

THEIR, THERE, THEY'RE

+ Good students submit **their** homework on time. (possessive)

+ **There** are too many deadlines to submit homework.

+ **They're** often too busy to submit their homework. (Combination of 'they' and 'are')

TO, TOO, TWO

+ I sent it **to** him. (preposition)

+ I like cricket **too**. (also)

+ I read **two** books this week. (number)

WARY, WEARY

+ I was **wary** of his promise to return with my money on Monday. (suspicious)

+ I was **weary** from studying all night for the examination. (tired)

Since English is not our primary language, we literally translate Hindi words into English. The following table lists some common examples of poor English translations. I avoid them.

Incorrect	Correct
Return back	Return
Reply back	Reply
Take back	Return
Go back	Return
Revert back	Revert
Answer back	Reply
Confirm back	Confirm
Refer below table	Refer to the table below
Repeat again	Repeat
Much more taller	Much taller
I enjoyed like anything	I really enjoyed
Can you open the lights?	Can you switch on the lights?
Can you close the light?	Can you switch off the light?

APPENDIX-E

Seven-Minute Exercise

The 12 exercises for the seven-minute exercise routine are shown below. High-intensity circuit training (HICT) uses our body weight for resistance training similar to Yoga. In addition to resistance, the exercise also helps the heart (cardiovascular exercises).

The Human Performance Institute (HPI) asks us to do each exercise for 30 seconds in a fast-paced manner. Most of us acquire and maintain appropriate intensity for 30 seconds.

HPI suggests following the exercise sequence in the order discussed below. The sequence ensures that the muscles are not tired. A healthy person should be able to do these exercises without any pain. If you experience pain, stop immediately and see a doctor. Many YouTube videos show each of these exercises clearly. You can tear out these pages from the book and use them as a quick reference.

Before beginning any exercise program, we need to determine if our bodies are healthy enough for it. This may include consulting with a doctor.

1. **Jumping jacks**—Standing, put your feet together with your hands at your sides. In one fluid motion, jump and raise your arms simultaneously so that your arms are above your head. Land with your feet apart. Immediately jump again but bring your hands down to your sides and land with your feet together. You have just completed one jumping jack. The arm motion will resemble a bird flapping its wings.

2. Wall sit—Place your back against a wall and lower yourself until your knees are close to a 90-degree angle. Remain in this position for 30 seconds.

3. Push-ups—Proper push-ups require unbent knees with the body in a straight line from heel to head. Hands should be placed slightly wider than shoulder-length apart. Elbows should be kept close but not touch the sides.

4. Abdominal crunch—Lie on your back with your knees slightly bent. Put your feet on the floor and about hip-width-distance apart. Keep your knees comfortably apart. Fold arms on your chest and tighten your abdominal muscles. Raise your head and shoulders off of the floor. Hold for three deep breaths, then return to starting position. Do not clasp your hands behind your head when doing crunches.

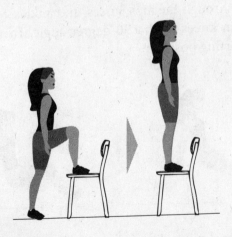

5. Step-up onto a chair—Step onto and off of a chair. Switch between legs each time. If you place your right foot on the chair first the first time, place your left foot on the chair first the second time.

6. Squat—Spread your feet apart, slightly greater than shoulder-width. Point your toes ahead. Slowly go down, bending through the hips, knees, and ankles. Stop when your knees reach a 90-degree angle. Then return to the starting position.

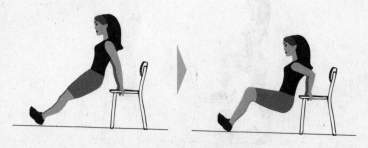

7. Triceps dip on chair—Sit on a bench or chair. Put your hands next to or slightly under your hips. Lift up onto your hands and bring your hips forward.

Bend your elbows (no lower than 90 degrees) and lower your hips down, keeping them very close to the chair. Keep your shoulders down. Push back up without locking the elbows and repeat.

8. Plank—Get into the push-up position. Rest on your forearms instead of your hands. Your elbows should line up under your shoulders. Bring your hands together. Hold this position.

9. High knees running in place—Run in place but lift your knees so that your thighs are perpendicular to your torso.

10. Lunge—Keeping your back straight with your hands on your hips, step forward with one leg and go down until your other knee nearly touches the ground. Alternate between legs each time.

11. Push-up and rotation—Begin in the push-up position, but as you come up, rotate your body so your right arm lifts up and points toward the ceiling. Your torso and arms should form a T. Return to the starting position, lower yourself, then push up and rotate till your left hand points toward the ceiling.

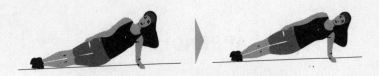

12. Side plank—Lie down on your side with your feet stacked on top of each other. Prop your upper body on your forearm. Place the non-support arm on your hip. Bring your hips off of the ground. Bring your body into as straight a line as possible. Keep your neck in neutral alignment as if you were comfortably standing.

APPENDIX-F

Saving Comparison Details

Jai invests for 8 years only, starts at age 22:

Years of investment	8 years
Investment amount	800,000
Total compound interest	23,094,087
Total maturity amount at the age of 65 years	23,894,087
Profit percentage (**29 times of the investment**)	2,887%

Age	Opening Balance	Investment Amount	Interest Rate	Compound Interest	Year-end Balance
22	0	100,000	8.7%	8,700	108,700
23	108,700	100,000	8.7%	18,157	226,857
24	226,857	100,000	8.7%	28,437	355,293
25	355,293	100,000	8.7%	39,611	494,904
26	494,904	100,000	8.7%	51,757	646,661
27	646,661	100,000	8.7%	64,959	811,620

28	811,620	100,000	8.7%	79,311	990,931
29	990,931	100,000	8.7%	94,911	1,185,842
30	1,185,842		8.7%	103,168	1,289,010
31	1,289,010		8.7%	112,144	1,401,154
32	1,401,154		8.7%	121,900	1,523,055
33	1,523,055		8.7%	132,506	1,655,560
34	1,655,560		8.7%	144,034	1,799,594
35	1,799,594		8.7%	156,565	1,956,159
36	1,956,159		8.7%	170,186	2,126,345
37	2,126,345		8.7%	184,992	2,311,337
38	2,311,337		8.7%	201,086	2,512,423
39	2,512,423		8.7%	218,581	2,731,004
40	2,731,004		8.7%	237,597	2,968,601
41	2,968,601		8.7%	258,268	3,226,869
42	3,226,869		8.7%	280,738	3,507,607
43	3,507,607		8.7%	305,162	3,812,769
44	3,812,769		8.7%	331,711	4,144,480
45	4,144,480		8.7%	360,570	4,505,049
46	4,505,049		8.7%	391,939	4,896,989
47	4,896,989		8.7%	426,038	5,323,027
48	5,323,027		8.7%	463,103	5,786,130
49	5,786,130		8.7%	503,393	6,289,523
50	6,289,523		8.7%	547,189	6,836,712
51	6,836,712		8.7%	594,794	7,431,506

52	7,431,506		8.7%	646,541	8,078,047
53	8,078,047		8.7%	702,790	8,780,837
54	8,780,837		8.7%	763,933	9,544,770
55	9,544,770		8.7%	830,395	10,375,165
56	10,375,165		8.7%	902,639	11,277,804
57	11,277,804		8.7%	981,169	12,258,973
58	12,258,973		8.7%	1,066,531	13,325,503
59	13,325,503		8.7%	1,159,319	14,484,822
60	14,484,822		8.7%	1,260,180	15,745,002
61	15,745,002		8.7%	1,369,815	17,114,817
62	17,114,817		8.7%	1,488,989	18,603,806
63	18,603,806		8.7%	1,618,531	20,222,337
64	20,222,337		8.7%	1,759,343	21,981,680
65	21,981,680		8.7%	1,912,406	23,894,087

Veeru invests for 35 years, starts at age 30:

Years of Investment	35 years
Investment amount	3,500,000
Total compound interest	20,317,130
Total maturity amount at the age of 65 years	23,817,130
Profit percentage **(5.8 times of the investment)**	580%

Age	Opening Balance	Invest-ment Amount	Inter-est Rate	Com-pound Interest	Year-end Balance
30	0	100,000	8.7%	8,700	108,700
31	108,700	100,000	8.7%	18,157	226,857
32	226,857	100,000	8.7%	28,437	355,293
33	355,293	100,000	8.7%	39,611	494,904
34	494,904	100,000	8.7%	51,757	646,661
35	646,661	100,000	8.7%	64,959	811,620
36	811,620	100,000	8.7%	79,311	990,931
37	990,931	100,000	8.7%	94,911	1,185,842
38	1,185,842	100,000	8.7%	111,868	1,397,710
39	1,397,710	100,000	8.7%	130,301	1,628,011
40	1,628,011	100,000	8.7%	150,337	1,878,348
41	1,878,348	100,000	8.7%	172,116	2,150,464
42	2,150,464	100,000	8.7%	195,790	2,446,255
43	2,446,255	100,000	8.7%	221,524	2,767,779
44	2,767,779	100,000	8.7%	249,497	3,117,276
45	3,117,276	100,000	8.7%	279,903	3,497,179
46	3,497,179	100,000	8.7%	312,955	3,910,133
47	3,910,133	100,000	8.7%	348,882	4,359,015
48	4,359,015	100,000	8.7%	387,934	4,846,949
49	4,846,949	100,000	8.7%	430,385	5,377,334
50	5,377,334	100,000	8.7%	476,528	5,953,862

51	5,953,862	100,000	8.7%	526,686	6,580,548
52	6,580,548	100,000	8.7%	581,208	7,261,755
53	7,261,755	100,000	8.7%	640,473	8,002,228
54	8,002,228	100,000	8.7%	704,894	8,807,122
55	8,807,122	100,000	8.7%	774,920	9,682,041
56	9,682,041	100,000	8.7%	851,038	10,633,079
57	10,633,079	100,000	8.7%	933,778	11,666,857
58	11,666,857	100,000	8.7%	1,023,717	12,790,573
59	12,790,573	100,000	8.7%	1,121,480	14,012,053
60	14,012,053	100,000	8.7%	1,227,749	15,339,802
61	15,339,802	100,000	8.7%	1,343,263	16,783,065
62	16,783,065	100,000	8.7%	1,468,827	18,351,891
63	18,351,891	100,000	8.7%	1,605,315	20,057,206
64	20,057,206	100,000	8.7%	1,753,677	21,910,883
65	21,910,883	100,000	8.7%	1,906,247	23,817,130

APPENDIX-G

Appearance

'You never get a second chance to make
a first impression.'
—WILL ROGERS
American humourist and social commentator

One day as the King was holding his court, a Swamiji came to see him. The King did not provide any special attention to the Swamiji. Eventually, the Swamiji's turn came. The King spoke to the Swamiji and was impressed by his wisdom. The King spent several hours with the Swamiji, seeking his knowledge on many subjects. When the Swamiji was leaving, the King got up from his throne and went to the gate to see him off.

The court ministers were surprised by the King's treatment of the Swamiji. They asked the King, 'When the Swamiji came, you did not pay any attention to him. However, when he was leaving, you went all the way to see him off. He was the same person, why did you treat him differently?'

To this question, the King replied, 'When the Swamiji came here, I judged him by his clothes *and appearance. As I talked to him, I realized his wisdom. I benefitted from his knowledge and blessings. Once I understood his wisdom, I treated him with due respect.'*

Since I did not attend a westernized high school, personal appearance was not explicitly discussed with me. I gained most of my knowledge by reading books on dressing, etiquette, and manners. I also observed how other successful people dressed. A simple and clean appearance is not expensive.

As a professional, I have an opportunity to dress the part. Some of my observations and mistakes are discussed below:

1. I now stay fit. I improved my looks, posture, and confidence with better fitness. Becoming fit was not easy. I had to work hard and it required a lot of discipline. Once I became fit, I began to notice people who were not fit. Whether we like it or not, many people view unfit or overweight people as undisciplined and lazy. In the long run, unfit people may have fewer opportunities.
2. Quit smoking cigarettes. Many people do not like the smell of smoke. Many smokers do not detect their own odour. I can. If I can, others definitely can smell your smoke. I realize quitting smoking is difficult. Smoking may be interpreted as a sign of a lack of discipline. This is unfair but many, including me, hold this opinion.

3. I keep my hair short, which offers a clean look and is easy to maintain. Since I have too much hair, I get a haircut every month. Many film actors try to develop a certain image through hair. Even when I was younger, I never tried to copy the hairstyle of Amitabh Bachchan or Shah Rukh Khan.

4. I shave every day despite the fact I do not enjoy shaving. Men should shave every day unless restricted by a religious preference (e.g., Muslim or Sikh). An unshaven look appears unclean.

5. I shave my moustache off completely. In the US, long hair and long moustaches were common in the 1970s. Now, I have a clean look.

6. I brush my teeth every day. I, and many others, notice poor teeth.

7. I take a bath every day before going to work. At IIT, we used to take a bath in the evening after classes due to water availability issues.

8. I do not use perfume. With closed air-conditioned (AC) offices, perfume is really apparent and distracting.

9. I sweat a lot so I use deodorant for my arm pits.

10. My fingernails are short.

11. I do not bite my nails.

12. Our dress code is business casual. I now watch how the high performers dress. They tend to represent the respected, not just accepted, dress code. I have mentioned poor dress to many

individuals. Clean and simple clothes are not expensive.

13. I always wear shoes to work and not sandals or chappal.

14. I am expected to match belt colour with shoe colour.

15. As our industry has advanced, I have begun wearing more formal shirts, which do not have wrinkles.

16. I do not wear earrings. Regardless of gender, experts suggest removing nose rings.

APPENDIX-H

Frequently-Asked Questions

Throughout the book, I avoided offering any advice. Readers are intelligent, and they can decide on their own. Instead, I shared my experiences and readers can draw their own conclusions.

When people ask me questions during my presentations, sometimes they are looking to confirm their decision or opinion. People tend to favour information that confirms their beliefs or hypotheses. Psychologists call this *Confirmation Bias*. With this bias, people interpret ambiguous evidence as supporting their existing position. I am sure that I have my own biases and ignore contradictory evidence. With this bias in mind, I answer the questions below:

1. I am in my final year of Engineering. Should I do an MBA instead of taking a job?

Speaking from experience, I worked for three years before I was accepted into a good MBA program. Work experience allowed me to better understand and relate to case studies and classroom discussions.

Even way back in 1986, one of my classmates at IIT was selected by IIM Calcutta right after his B.Tech. He declined the IIM Calcutta offer. He said he would first gain useful work experience for 2 years and then reappear for the entrance examination at IIM Calcutta. My classmate chose to work for 2 years in the automobile industry. He was accepted again by IIM Calcutta

In the 1980s, MBA slots in IIMs were very limited. It was unusual for anyone to wait for 2 years. He did. In today's world, with additional MBA options, take a long-term view. I encourage most students to gain work experience before deciding if they want to do an MBA.

2. Should I take an OK job in a dream company or a dream job in an OK company?

Most people select a dream job in an OK company. I have seen people do better if they join an entrepreneurial company. If the company is doing well, the company will have more opportunities than leaders. They will offer new challenges and employees can rise. If the company is sinking or shrinking, the opportunities are going to be more limited every year.

3. Should I pursue an MBA from a good school or do a Master's in Engineering in the US?

The answer depends on your immediate interest. Very few people do both. I am one of them. I advise people to do an MBA only from a good college (top 20). I do not suggest doing an MBA just for the sake of doing an MBA. As mentioned earlier, proper skills are what employers want. Master's programs (MBA and MS) are one way to gain those skills. Many successful people in our company never attended a formal Master's program.

4. How should I choose between two job offers? Low salary with more learning opportunities or higher salary with fewer learning opportunities?

I always suggest choosing learning opportunities. Your salary will improve in the long run.

5. I do not like to exercise. How can I change?

I also do not like to exercise. I find exercise boring and painful while I am doing it. However, I feel much better in the long run. Personally, I found that I enjoy playing badminton. So I play that sport on a regular basis. If I enjoy a sport, I am likely to stay with it.

6. I like to spend money. As a result, I do not save any money. How can I save?

Systematic Investment Plan (SIP) and other similar schemes are a great way to save. Experts suggest 'pay yourself first' every month. If money is withdrawn automatically from my salary account and deposited to my SIP account, I cannot overspend.

7. Is there a 'mantra' or shortcut to success?

Yes. Since we are living our life for the first time, we are amateurs. Avoid playing the 'loser's game' and do everything with a deliberate purpose.

8. I do great work as an engineer. Why should anyone care about my clothes or appearance?

Just like our body, we want all of the body parts to work properly. One area may not be as strong. Similarly, most companies want us to maintain minimum standards in each area of our presence. Once we meet the minimum standards in every area, we can focus and excel in a few areas.

9. I do not like to read. How can I learn?

Reading books is one of the lowest cost ways of learning. Other techniques include audio tapes (podcasts) or videos (YouTube). We can attend classes where someone is giving a lecture. We can start a discussion or study group within our company.

10. I do not like my job or my manager. What should I do?

Assuming that you like your company and the industry, I suggest working to identify areas of your job that you enjoy more. In my experience, 85 percent of the daily work in most jobs in most companies is routine and repetitive. Only about 15 percent of the work is new or different. If work was fun, most companies would not have to pay people to do it. Just like fun parks, people would pay to work. Experts suggest that areas that we enjoy more are probably related to our strengths. If we seek additional assignments in those areas, we likely will come out ahead in the long run.

As far as the manager is concerned, probably the feeling is mutual. Probably your manager does not dislike you. She probably just does not appreciate your habits and behaviours. Every person has their own unique work style. Some managers are more responsive to people needs while others are reserved and do not talk much. Some other managers are direct, demanding, and decisive. Once you understand the manager as a person, you can adjust your work style to meet your manager's needs.

11. I like my current job. I want to move to a city near my hometown. I am unable to find a similar job in a city of my choice. What should I do?

I chose professional growth and opportunities over living close to my family. In the new scheme (dhancha), most good job opportunities are limited to six or seven metros. If both you and your spouse work, it is unlikely that you will find two great jobs in a small city for the 40 years of your work life. We have to be prepared to move to another large city for professional reasons.

Notes

1. John P. Kotter, *The New Rules: How to Succeed in Today's Post-Corporate World* (Simon and Schuster, 1995).
2. Jim Collins, *Good to Great: Why Some Companies Make the Leap...and Others Don't* (Harper Collins, 2001).
3. Thomas Friedman, *The Lexus and the Olive Tree: Understanding Globalization* (Picador, 2012).
4. Peter Diamandis explains why we can look forward to abundance in our future in his inspiring TED talk. http://www.ted.com/talks/peter_diamandis_abundance_is_our_future.html
5. http://articles.economictimes.indiatimes.com/2013-04-02/news/38218110_1_engineering-colleges-india-big-draw
6. http://www.rediff.com/getahead/slide-show/slide-show-1-career-only-10-percent-mbas-employable/20130131.htm#1
7. Julie Bick, *All I Really Need To Know In Business I Learned At Microsoft: Insider Strategies To Help You Succeed* (New York: Pocket Books, 1997), p. 150.

8. For a well-written story on multitasking, see: Dave Crenshaw, *The Myth of Multitasking: How 'Doing it All' Gets Nothing Done* (San Francisco: Jossey-Bass, 2008).

9. Edward M. Hallowell, M.D., *CrazyBusy: Overstretched, Overbooked, and About to Snap!* (New York: Ballantine Books, 2006).

10. http://www.cbsnews.com/8301-504763_162-57357895-10391704/internet-addiction-changes-brain-similar-to-cocaine-study/

11. For more research on distractions, see: Keller and Papsan, *The One Thing: The Surprisingly Simple Truth Behind Extraordinary Results* (Austin: Bard Press, 2012).

12. See also: Paul Glen, *Leading Geeks: How to Manage and Lead the People Who Deliver Technology* (Jossey-Bass, 2002), pp. 86-87.

13. http://www.linkedin.com/today/post/article/20130506104243-86541065-how-graduates-can-get-ahead

14. For members in the human resources department, please see this illuminating quote from a book I highly recommend. 'That is, HR professionals almost invariably define *business* as 'HR business' and are inclined to talk about their current initiatives in leadership training, recruiting, engagement, or rewards—the areas where they focus their attention on the job. These efforts are important but they are not *the business*. They are in support of the business.

    The real business is external: the context and setting in which the business operates, the expectations of key stakeholders (customers, investors, communities, partners, employees, and so forth), and the strategies that give a company a unique competitive advantage.'

David Ulrich, Jon Younger, Wayne Brockbank, and Mike Ulrich, *HR from the Outside In: Six Competencies for the Future of Human Resources* (New York: McGraw-Hill, 2012), p. 7.

15. I was introduced to Locus of Control by Gazelles, Inc., an executive education firm. More details about Locus of Control available at https://en.wikipedia.org/wiki/Locus_of_control

16. Jo Owen, *The Leadership Skills Handbook: 50 Key Skills from 1,000 Leaders* (London: Kogan, 2006), p. 25.

17. Robert Bolton and Dorothy Grover Bolton, *People Styles at Work and Beyond* (American Management Association, 2009).

18. Stephen R. Covey, *The Seven Habits of Highly Effective People* (Free Press, 2004).

19. http://www.businessweek.com/magazine/content/09_26/b4137000552758.htm

20. Effectively prioritizing applies to all areas of life. For a good book see: David Allen, *Making It All Work: Winning at the Game of Work and the Business of Life* (New York: Penguin, 2008).

21. http://online.wsj.com/article/SB10001424127887324520904578551462766909232.html

22. Justin Kruger and David Dunning, 'Unskilled and Unaware of It: How Difficulties in Recognizing One's Own Incompetence Lead to Inflated Self-Assessments,' *Psychology* 1 (2009), pp. 30–46. https://www.math.ucdavis.edu/~suh/metacognition.pdf

23. The *New York Times* article accurately describes our challenges because of inactive lifestyle and easy availability of fried food and sweets everywhere. http://india.blogs.nytimes.com/2013/01/29/ fighting-fat-at-india-inc-one-dosa-at-a-time/

24. The tomato is a great fruit. Since we use tomato for cooking, many of us refer to it as a vegetable. Read more about the fruit at http://en.wikipedia.org/wiki/ Tomato

25. The University of Maryland Medical Center recommends eating tomatoes to help prevent kidney stones. http://umm.edu/health/medical/altmed/ condition/kidney-stones

26. Professor Robert H. Lustig, M.D. has made a strong case for avoiding sugar, a processed food that causes obesity and disease. I strongly encourage you to take 90 minutes to watch this video. http://www. youtube.com/watch?v=dBnniua6-oM

27. http://journals.lww.com/acsm-healthfitness/ Fulltext/2013/05000/HIGH_INTENSITY_ CIRCUIT_TRAINING_USING_BODY_ WEIGHT_.5.aspx#

28. http://www.ifa.com/pdf/EllisCharlesThe_Loser's_ Game1975.pdf

29. See also: Charles Ellis, *Winning the Loser's Game: Timeless Strategies for Successful Investing* 6th Edition (McGraw-Hill, 2013).

30. Jim Collins and Morten T. Hansen, *Great By Choice: Uncertainty, Chaos, and Luck – Why Some Thrive Despite Them All* (New York: Harper Business, 2011).

31. Jim Collins and Jerry Porras, *Built to Last: Successful Habits of Visionary Companies* (Harper Collins, 1997).

32. Stephen Covey, *The SPEED of Trust: The One Thing That Changes Everything* (Simon & Schuster Inc., 2006).

33. Geoff Smart and Randy Street, *Who: The A Method for Hiring* (Ballantine Books, 2008).

34. Marcus Buckingham and Curt Coffman, *First, Break All the Rules: What the World's Great Managers Do Differently* (Simon & Schuster, 1999).

35. Robert Bolton and Dorothy Grover Bolton, *People Styles at Work and Beyond* (American Management Association, 2009).

36. Michael Watkins, *The First 90 Days: Critical Success Strategies for New Leaders at All Levels* (Harvard Business School Press, 2003).

37. Michael Armstrong, *How to Be An Even Better Manager: A Complete A to Z of Proven Techniques and Essential Skills* (Kogan Page, 2011).

38. Bradberry and Greaves, *Emotional Intelligence 2.0.*

39. Mehmet C. Oz, M.D., and Michael F. Roizen, M.D., *You: The Owner's Manual. An Insider's Guide to the Body That Will Make You Healthier* (Harper Collins, 2008).

40. Jack Canfield, *The Success Principles: How to Get from Where You Are to Where You Want to Be* (Harper Collins, 2005).